Also by Neil Stannard

Piano Technique Demystified:
Insights into Problem Solving, 2nd Edition 2014

The Pianist's Guide to Practical Technique
111 Technical Studies from Music You Want to Play, Complete, 2014

The Pianist's Guide to Practical Technique:
111 Technical Studies from Music You Want to Play
Volume I, Numbers 1-55, 2014

The Pianist's Guide to Practical Technique:
111 Technical Studies from Music You Want to Play
Volume II, Numbers 56-111, 2014

Guided Sight-Reading Practice at the Piano:
Four-Hand Excursions for Teacher and Student
(Early to Late Intermediate), 2014

The Art of the Fugue *by J.S. Bach:*
More Sight-Reading Practice
Intermediate to Advanced, 2014

The Pianist's Guide to Practical Scales and Arpeggios:
As They Occur in Pieces You Want to Play, 2015

15 Sinfonias for String Trio by J.S. Bach, 2015

11 Fugues and 2 Preludes for String Trio by J.S. Bach. 2015

Mystified No More

Further Insights
Into Piano Technique

NEIL STANNARD

ISBN-13: 978-1517643256
ISBN-10: 1517643252

CONTENTS

MUSICAL EXAMPLES

"No one ever told me you could choose where to be on the keyboard."

Unlike life, playing the piano continues to be easy and still doesn't hurt.

INTRODUCTION
Toward a Practical Technique

Knowledge is a wonderful thing. Have you ever noticed, though, that the more you have, the more you seem to need? Once someone opens that window of insight, the drive to have a closer look can be compelling.

Since the appearance of *Piano Technique Demystified: Insights into Problem Solving*, 2nd edition, emails from around the world have found their way to my inbox, asking for more specific details in particular repertoire. Combined with the continuing issues brought to me by my own students, these questions inspire me to offer another volume of insights into problem solving. Here we consider in more detail how principles explained in the first volume can be applied to a variety of technical and musical issues as they occur in repertoire.

In the previous volume we learned how to use the body according to its design. We learned that it is more efficient to move than to stretch to an extreme and how to make decisions regarding fingering. We learned how to "get after" a passage and to play "honestly." We learned that mindless-rote is more likely to produce technical vagaries than reliable passage work. Perhaps most importantly we learned that if a passage doesn't feel easy, then we haven't solved it.

A practical technique is one in which practicing takes place on purpose. The brain is engaged at all times and connected to the physical response, asking at every technical turn, "does this feel easy?" A practical technique absorbs solutions to problems in repertoire, knowing that if used according to its design, the body will provide. So, treat the topics in this book as individual brainteasers. Try the examples and work them in carefully as instructed. If there is particular repertoire you want to explore, then look for those examples; it is not necessary to tackle each chapter in order. Don't be intimidated by some repertoire that seems more virtuose than that to which you are accustomed. The technical principles can be applied to any repertoire.

You will notice in these essays some overlap with *Piano Technique Demystified*. It is my hope this overlap will provide more depth into the various concepts that, when combined, contribute to an efficient technique. Technical suggestions are not necessarily comprehensive. There can sometimes be more than one solution to a problem depending on the needs of a particular pianist. The solutions presented, though, demonstrate uses of the foremost principles of an efficient technique, one that takes into consideration the design of the body: forearm rotation, shaping, grouping, fingering and other concepts. Sometimes we find conflicting principles when considering a particular problem. In this case, choose the one that feels easier. There will always be a clear choice.

I selected the examples from a wide range of repertoire, intermediate to advanced. My hope is that the concepts will become second nature, enough so that even if a particular work is not in the fingers, the processes of how to get it there will become clearer. In order to further clarify, knowing as I do that words often fail, I include links to iDemos.

They Didn't Teach Piano

Juilliard's Rosina Lhevinne was the renown mentor of John Browning, Garrick Ohlsson, Van Cliburn and many others who became household names in the mid-twentieth century. But she didn't teach piano. She said so. I have it on good authority that she would be more likely to ask a student what concerto he learned over the weekend. Madame Lhevinne was more of a coach-consultant than someone who would (or could?) show a student how to move from one note to the next. Lhevinne's successor reportedly threw a score at someone with a technical problem, certain that would be the perfect solution.

Lhevinne and her successor were right in a way. Serious students must come prepared. But the old-fashioned notion that a student performs for the teacher is not particularly helpful. In a performance, the objective is to make music and disguise technical deficiency. As much as I enjoy a fine performance, when a student comes to me I want her to reveal the problems, if any, so we can solve them together.

I advise my students to prepare as follows: If a passage doesn't feel easy, even if it sounds great, there must be a technical reason why it isn't working, and that is what we should discuss. In other words, bring questions. Having said that, there is certainly a time for performance, and that time can be anytime a student wants to try out a piece, to find out how it feels to play it through no matter what. This can also reveal topics for discussion. Finally, though, the technical work will produce a performance at some level. It is possible to work so much on technical details that the music gets lost. This we want to avoid.

In my studio I teach piano, and the lessons in this book are a reflection of that policy. Think of each essay and its examples as lessons on how to solve technical problems, the point of which is to make music with ease and efficiency at the highest level possible. Think of them as your own private piano lessons, during which you can solve problems, work the solutions up to tempo and run trial performances. Knowing how it is that you do what you do is the objective. There is really nothing more satisfying than that.

[Editor's Note: Video demonstrations (iDemos) of selected musical examples may be found by typing into your web browser the URL http://tinyurl.com/Mystified-Examples. They are listed in numerical order in the playlist called "Mystified No More" and identified here in the text with ♪.]

I
WORKING THE PIANO

What's in a Word?

Pianists, like ballerinas and circus acrobats, try their best to hide the work they do. When the house lights dim and the moment of truth arrives, rehearsing becomes a distant memory, and only the performance, with maybe a touch of perspiration, remains. It all seems effortless. Performers can do something that most people can't, and we make it look easy, which I suppose is why the public takes it for granted.

These thoughts popped into my head as I rounded the familiar corner off University Avenue toward the rear drive of Clark House, Mecca for music students. Pitched gables of the Victorian mansion drew my eyes upward and I marveled at the persistence of this once grand house, weathered and drab now, but like an aristocrat with more pedigree than cash, seemed to accept its fate with grace. Inside, I would learn what a difference a word can make.

I squeezed myself into a narrow perch at one corner of the grand drawing room, the largest of three on the main floor and watched a gaggle of piano majors file in, chattering easily as students do on the first day of a class—no class history yet, no assignments due, a clean slate. An up-chin nod from an acquaintance or a friendly wave "hey" eased the vague sense of dread that occupied my thoughts recently. My teacher called it the junior blues.

It was the first week of the fall semester, 1963, the beginning of my junior year. I still reeled from the sudden death on registration day a week earlier of Muriel Kerr, my piano teacher. I noticed that the Steinway stood open and ready at the front of the room, framed by ornate bay windows flanked on either side by richly carved bookcases with leaded-glass doors. It was the audition piano, the one I played for Kerr. Through the window I could see a large evergreen, and beyond that across deep lawns a low wall of sundry stone and mortar separated us from the traffic on Adams Boulevard. It seemed odd to me that life would continue as planned, despite the untimely death of Muriel Kerr, who left me with a question dangling: What did she mean when she told me to "get after that!"? Here we were, though, on the first day of piano lit, attempting to proceed with the doings of ordinary life on an ordinary day.

I don't remember much about the content of that first class except that Beethoven's second concerto was played by a graduate student named David, his premature baldness drawing light from an overhead chandelier as if the Tiffany-encased globes were the source of his power. We learned that the second concerto was actually first in order of composition, something I filed away as further evidence that things are not always as they at first appear.

I remember a sturdy performance, quite effortful it seemed, as sweat dripped down the back of the David's neck and along the bridge of his nose, a

1

precarious situation for his horn-rimmed glasses. Sound took on a physical presence in the room along with the students, drawing the paneled walls inward and giving me a sense that the room was much too small for the lot of us. Afterward, in the ensuing discussion, David made a comment that has stuck with me all these years. "I don't *play* the piano," he said, "I *work* the piano."

The words *play* and *work* began to rattle around in my brain. Even then, in the dark ages of my technical development, I had an inkling of conflicting connotations and denotations. There were some giggles from the class and not a few nods in agreement as he spoke. My mind flashed on certain passages in the Chopin Ballade Kerr assigned me the previous spring, and I had to agree. If appearances can be trusted at all, David did indeed seem to be working hard when he played. But as he spoke to us from his stance in the curve of the piano, drawing himself up to his full five-feet eight, I sensed in his manner—the set of his mouth and the way he cupped his hands as if about to sing an aria—that he had something else in mind. I didn't know yet what it was.

Working as Opposed to Playing?

Example 1. Chopin Ballade Op. 47. Work.

When I first tackled the A-flat Ballade, certain passages did indeed seem like work (example 1). At the time, I took this to be the norm. I know better now. It was on the occasion of an outing of this Ballade in the presence of Miss Kerr that she suggested I "get after that." I didn't have a clue what she meant, though I was fairly sure it had something to do with how hard I was working.

I never had the chance to ask her how to make the passage less like work. Now, though, I have some answers. This passage has several issues in play—so to speak. Let's consider the leaping right-hand sixteenths (example 2 ♪). The

Example 2. Chopin Ballade Op. 47. Answers ♪.

brackets in measures one and three indicate groups. As you do doubt remember from *Piano Technique Demystified*, notes can be grouped together to facilitate execution, the last note of one group sending the hand to the first note of the next group. (Thus endeth the review.) The dotted arrows simulate the throwing of the hand by means of rotation to the next group. The potential danger here, the trap I may have fallen into, was perhaps twofold—I didn't understand how to use my thumb to rotate to the chord and, because of that, I probably kept my hand too open. This is hard work, indeed.

Notice my right-hand fingering in measure two; it is different from the Paderewski edition. Notice, too, that I take the E and F-sharp at the end of the measure with the left hand. This is much more facile for the average to smallish hand and less likely to produce crashing into mountains of black keys.

When I first studied this piece all I knew to do was practice slowly and repeatedly. Now I know to first work-in these mechanical details in brief units, one group at a time, gradually increasing the speed. During this process of cranking up the tempo—a phrase coined by my students—the group continues to feel easy at each new tempo.

The next item for discussion is that leaping left hand (example 3 ♪). Group from short to long, eighth to quarter. Use the fifth finger as a hinge from which to rotate leftward, falling back to the right for thumb and octave. The feeling is very much like moving from five on the E to thumb on the C-natural. At the end of measure two I spell out a more convenient redistribution of notes.

Example 3. Chopin Ballade Op. 47. Leaping LH ♪.

In the heat of the moment, we sometimes forget that *arpeggiated* chords need to have a place in time—like all ornaments indicated with a symbol, as in measure four of example one. We mustn't throw ourselves at them like ungainly school children. Here is how I manage rolled chords (example 4):

Example 4. Chopin Ballade Op. 47. LH *Arpeggios*.

The following passage (example 5 ♪) is one of those seemingly endless harmonic and melodic sequences, the function of which is to delay. It gives us a prolonged suspension of forward motion harmonically, while at the same time seeming to move excitedly forward. Through a series of secondary dominants, each of which cancels out the preceding sonority, we arrive back pretty much where we started, on the dominate of E major, a key with which we had been flirting when we started—a courtship but no actual proposal.

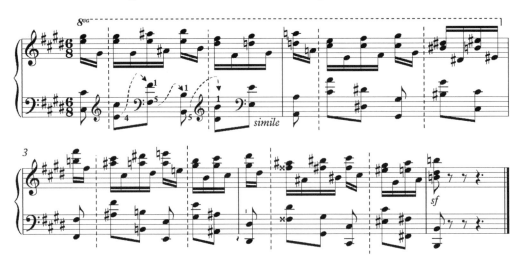

Example 5. Chopin Ballade Op. 47. Sequence ♪.

Call me shallow, but I always fall for a sequence. This one I found particularly captivating because of its bravura and, well, it never seems to stop. The pitfall for me at that time was my tendency to play through, over and over, without considering the technical details. This passage was work. In my defense, when so completely smitten my mind floods with emotion and anything goes.

One afternoon I grabbed a chance to run through the passage before class on the Steinway in the same parlor where David had been speaking. I was alone and the door was closed. Suddenly, the door flung open and in strode two of my classmates, shouting "endless sequence, be gone" and "such decadence." I won't mention any names, but the latter of the two became a well-known conductor whose initials are MTT. At that time MTT would only consider playing Bach and anything twentieth century, especially Stravinsky. (I once heard him secretly practicing "Ondine," though, but you didn't hear it from me.) Now he is celebrated for his interpretations of Mahler. We all grow.

The passage seemed to be working fine technically—until the rude interruption. Once I felt a distraction—an awareness of surroundings—I lost track, not of the notes, but how they felt in my hands. I thought about that later in the practice room, but I only knew to repeat slowly.

Here's what I now know. Notice after each dashed vertical line the hands move outward in contrary motion (example 5). As we know, since the hands are mirror images of each other, they feel as if they are performing the same task when doing opposites. Here, though, it is the shape of the line that feels the same, not the individual techniques. Notice how the left hand seems to leap wildly hither and yon, excited as it is to travel through so much harmonic territory—outlining root positions to boot. Forget about the hither and yon and concentrate on using each chord to propel the hand to each succeeding chord by means of rotation. Notice that the dashed arrows in the first leap indicate a connection between the fourth finger and the thumb to which it rotates. Continue in similar fashion.

The right hand sallies forward almost casually by means of single rotation (changing direction with each note) as it makes its own shapes, taking into consideration relationships of black to white keys. Feel a very tiny bit more weight on the chords as they lead the way upward. Figure out each hand separately one group at a time. Then go ahead, throw caution to the wind and send the hands out into the world. I'm sure they'll play nicely together.

It's About Semantics

If I implement the above technical strategies does this constitute *playing*? Or am I still *working*, albeit with knowledge? David said he didn't *play* the piano but that he *worked* the piano. And what the class assumed was that what we do is difficult, the music requires physical strain. From what I could see of his performance the connotation of *work* did indeed have to do with effort. As it turned out, though, his meaning was quite different.

David meant to convey his dismay over the public's *perception* of what we do. Because we appear to know what we're doing, usually, and make it seem easy, the audience tends to assume that it isn't really all that serious—it's play, not a serious vocation, not work. It's something to be taken for granted. "Oh, you play the piano? Strum us out a tune."

Fritz Kreisler, the great violin virtuoso of the early twentieth century, so the story goes, once was invited to dine. Mrs. Upper Eastside was so effusive, wouldn't he please come to dinner—is there a Mrs. Kreisler? Oh, do bring her as well. We'll have such a lovely time. Just as she was about to ring off, she added, and oh, Mr. Kreisler, do bring your violin. To which the master answered succinctly, and I'm sure without malice, "Regrettably, madam, my violin does not dine."

The Glamorous Life

Over the years I've collected experiences of my own supporting David's inclination to change the rhetoric from *playing the piano* to *working the piano*. I have learned to make the effort—the *work*—technically easy, more like what I would call *play*. Even so, I got David's meaning as I embarked on a performing career, a vocation that, as often as not, seemed not to be taken seriously, not considered a legitimate route to the production of one's bread and butter.

One evening after a trio program my colleagues and I joined members of the presenting committee for the usual reception afterwards, they in their Sunday best, and we in our work clothes—formal dress. We got the usual questions: Where did you perform last night? Where do you go from here? Who is married to whom (meaning, who's sleeping with whom)? What is it like in New York? How do you like our town? Then, up comes Mrs. Car Dealer. I stand balancing a plate in one hand, a partially nibbled sandwich listing precariously at the edge, and in my other hand a plastic cup filled with something red. No hands free for greeting, so I nod and smile my friendly— hopefully not weary— smile. Now remember, I have just played for two hours and I stand before Mrs. Car Dealer in my white tie and tails. After the requisite questions, she looks up at me with a puzzled face, and asks—well-meaning, I'm sure, "Now, Mr. Stannard, what is it that you do?"

Another time, after a concert early in my career I had an introduction to the glamorous life of the touring artist. I called David in Los Angeles from my hotel in Sioux City or Sioux Falls—or was it St. Joseph or St. Cloud? Let's see, there was a town-square with the J.C. Penny on one corner and opposite diagonally a Sears and Roebuck. In the center stood an ersatz Romanesque town hall of Venetian-red sandstone, and the concert took place in the high school auditorium if it was pre-war, or in a gymnasium, divided in the center by sliding partitions. Oh wait, that could have been nearly any of the towns where Roz and I played that winter.

Rosalind Hupp-Hayes sang at the Metropolitan Opera. She had the noble bearing of one of the Valkyries she portrayed, but without the stereotypical heft. In place of the horned helmet sat a rather convincing facsimile of a diamond tiara. When she sang, her dark contralto enveloped you with a richness that could protect you from all evil—and possibly the ice storm outside. At intermission she changed into excessive yardage of emerald green taffeta whose folds and facets caught the light, fashioned it into gemstones of splendid hues and hurled them back into the darkened theater. This was a gown so stunning the audience gasped when she emerged from the wings back into the footlights. We were a hit.

I told David it had happened to me already, on my first professional tour, the confusion of *work* and *play*.

"Here we are after the concert," I began, hoping to paint an accurate picture. "Roz in her elaborate gown and tiara. I'm in my tails and white tie. We wait a bit backstage for someone to come fetch us—usually there's a reception at someone's house or in the cafeteria."

"Where are you," he laughed.

"Not sure, but listen—nobody comes to get us, so we give up and start to leave. We're hungry, you know, after a concert…so, we head out down one hallway only to find the gate has been pulled shut and padlocked. We can't get out."

I hear him laughing at the other end of the line.

"It's not funny. We're tired and hungry. This is supposed be a glamorous life."

"So what'd you do?"

"We wandered down another hall until we found a custodian. He seemed pretty startled to see us, but he had a key. He watched us make our way into the parking lot, Roz hiking her yardage to the knees, as we slogged to our car through patches of yesterday's weather. I was glad I opted not to get the patent leather shoes. The moon shone from high, giving us ample light, and I had forgotten about stars and how sharp they can be in crisp winter air away from the city."

"Well, you got out."

"Wait, wait. That's not the end. We drove out onto the state highway hoping to find a place to get something. The only place we find looks promising, a club of some sort. So we go in, right? We're dressed like the top of a wedding cake. The waitress does a double take, 'Shooee,' she says. 'Where y'all been?' I tell her we just played a concert and would like something to eat. 'Shucks, honey, the kitchen's closed. I can get y'all somethin' from the bar?'"

"We decide that's at least a start. So she puts us in a booth back in a dark corner of the restaurant section, next to the kitchen door. We're the only ones. The walls appear to be flocked with something fuzzy and probably red, though it's too dark to tell. The only light comes from a flicker in a small round globe with a votive candle, and from an archway leading from the bar shone a faint shaft of neon."

"'So what's the concert,' she says with a good-natured grin as she plants her groin against the table. She has the biggest hair I've ever seen, decorated with little sequins that would probably sparkle given half a chance. 'I love music,' she continues. 'I can play the guitar a little, but not so as to make a concert, y'all know what I mean?' She blushes at this. 'So what kind of concert?' I offered the briefest explanation I could think of—she sings, I play the piano. 'Oh,' she rises up on the toes of her sensible shoes. 'I luuuv the piano. My little sister used to take, you know, before, well, when momma made her do it. But she played in church because she could chord, yes she did.' Then her face brightened, and she leaned into me as if we were intimate friends. She gestured toward a wizened upright skulking in the shadows, its toothy grin marred by the absence of several ivories. 'Strum us out a tune?'"

I could tell David was about to lose it. Before he could speak, though, I continued.

"Here's an image I'd like to leave you with," I said. "We still haven't eaten, right? So as we exit the club I make a wrong turn onto the highway. Roz is really good-natured about this, so she says just go on a bit—maybe we'll find something. And sure enough, not far up ahead is one of those big trucker signs casting its fuzzy-edged beacon shimmering into the night air, totally obliterating the stars: 24-Hour Truck Stop. Well, we go in and step up to the counter. After the ultramarine sky outside, the brilliance of the interior was like—well, it was like being back on stage. The only two booths have burly-looking men in assorted sizes and colors, unshaven and looking the worse for wear. They glance everywhere but at each other. For a moment I think we've wandered into a Hopper painting. I can feel their eyes on us as we negotiate the revolving stools. Roz steadies her tiara with one hand and tries to spread her voluminous skirt over the seat with the other, but the seat keeps spinning and she can't sit down. I put my arms around her waist and help steady her down onto it and hop up next to her, flipping my tails out from under as if I were seated at the piano. There were plenty of stares, but no one said a word to us. Best of all, they didn't have a piano."

Creators or Re-creators?

My colleagues and I enjoyed those experiences and laugh about the craziness of some of the quirks attached to a performing career. Performing one night in a big city with a "Carnegie Hall" and the next night somewhere in the heartland—in a high school gym or *cafetorium*—could be a humbling experience. Nevertheless, no matter how the audience perceived our vocation, we always took our work seriously—not unlike monks in a faraway land who argue how many angels can dance on the head of a pin.

I have heard it said that what we do is self-indulgent public exhibitionism, that we are a class of show-offs. Some say that our work, our performing, is an act of re-creation, that performers are only interpreters; others say performing is a creative art worthy of its own classification. It seems to me that without the score, the composer's creation, there wouldn't be anything to interpret. But without the performers there wouldn't be any music. If a performer takes this:

Example 6. Bach Choral. Figured Bass.

and produces this:

Example 7. Bach Chorale. Harmonized.

what has transpired? Is this an act of creation or re-creation? How much of a leap, then, would it be to compare this:

Example 8. Schumann Op. 15, "From Foreign Lands and People."

with this?:

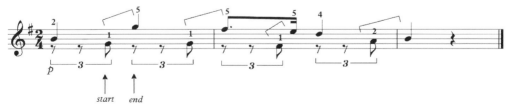

Example 9. Schumann "From Foreign Lands and People." As Played ♪.

Just to clarify, example nine shows what happens technically when preparing example eight for performance. Compare these two Mozart examples:

Example 10. Mozart K. 545. As Written.

Example 11. Mozart K. 545. As Played ♪.

Notice in example 11 (♪) how we prepare the performance by grouping notes for technical ease, as indicated by brackets. Feel a starting place after the first sixteenth. Mozart created a harmonic structure, in this case blocked chords, but leaves it to us performers to manage the realization. Notice, too, how we make musical decisions regarding articulation.

We performers are creators. We create a performance from a plan created by the composer. See how in example twelve—by re-dividing and choreographing the hands, grouping and changing fingering—I've created a performance of the Tchaikovsky Concerto[1]:

Example 12. Tchaikovsky Concerto As Created By Stannard.

We *work* the piano in order to *play* music; if playing music is our vocation, then *playing* the piano is our work. If you're getting a headache, I understand. It doesn't really matter whether we performers are in a particular category; what matters is that we learn to play with ease and take our work seriously.

---

[1] For more on this see my article "On Practicing the Piano" in the February/March edition of *American Music Teacher.*

Leave it to the faraway monks to decide if performers create or recreate. And it matters not at all whether our audiences think performing is a legitimate occupation as long as we do. One of my former roommates told a story about a private concert he played in a fancy, well-appointed home. They specifically asked for Hindemith's complete *Ludus Tonalis*. Afterwards, Madam arose from her throne of silk damask, waddled ever so daintily across her splendid Isfahan carpet and handed him ten dollars—sort of an afterthought. My friend was so insulted—he's a Quaker, you know, and non-confrontational—so his response was surprising. "Oh, no,'" he said handing the bill back to her, "take the money and have your piano tuned."

Some years ago I heard that Clark House, that old aristocratic Victorian mansion, had finally given way to the bulldozer and been buttered under to become a parking lot. I've no idea what happened to the fixtures, the tiffany shades and leaded-glass doors. Maybe the carved panels found a new home, where on a quite summer evening some faint echo of the glory days could resonate still. I was told they carefully dismantled the small upstairs studio in the northwest corner where the great Jascha Heifetz received his violin students. That, sadly, turned out not to be the case. It was his home studio that became part of the Colburn School in downtown Los Angeles. All that is left, then, of the locale of that fall in 1963, the September of Muriel Kerr's death and the semester of my junior blues, is what those of us who were there have taken away with us.

II
GEOGRAPHY OF THE KEYBOARD
Location, Location, Location

Who Knew?

Susan paused abruptly while playing a passage we had been discussing. A pianist of considerable experience, she was new to my studio, and I expected she wanted to ask another question. She stared for several seconds at the expanse of keyboard real estate before her as if considering where to stake a claim. She then looked up at me, her face a puzzle of conflicting emotions, and said, "No one ever told me that you could choose where to be on the keyboard."

I would have taken this to be a joke, except for the odd expression on her face. I saw there a reflection of her dismay. Where to be on the keyboard at any given time—a crucial bit of information—had not come up in her previous instruction, and I realized that her dismay was compounded by the fact that she had never even thought to ask about it. A slight tugging about the corners of her mouth, though, told me she was glad and maybe a touch relived. Mystery solved.

String players know that there is only one optimal location to place a finger on the string in order to produce a particular pitch. But we pianists have, comparatively speaking, a vast expanse of real estate to deal with, eighty-eight keys that represent acreage of pre-determined plots that we can depress at any point to produce the desired pitch. How many students, I wonder, ever learn that there is good reason to explore this territory, to become intimately acquainted with the hills and valleys, to teach the fingers the easiest and most efficient access points? This begs the question, is there an optimal location to depress the key? And if so, where is it?

The Physics

Piano keys are levers. We recall from high school physics that a lever balances at a hinge point, a fulcrum, and that depressing the lever at a point farthest from the fulcrum produces maximum control—like a seesaw. This spot is near the end of the piano key, at the outermost edge. I describe this as being *out*, toward the player's torso. Notice in example 13 (♪) that it is possible to play out, toward the edges of the keys when all keys are white, especially if it is understood that the favorite disposition of the thumb is to play in the *direction* of *in*. This means that the thumb, too, can play at the outer edge as it moves inwardly. Said another way, the thumb's normal position when not playing is often in space, not over the keyboard. Yes, I mean dangling in front of the keys. This flies in the face of some early instructions to children along the lines of "every finger [and thumb] lives in its own little house," a concept that must later be unlearned. At best the fingers are itinerant and the thumb is virtually homeless.

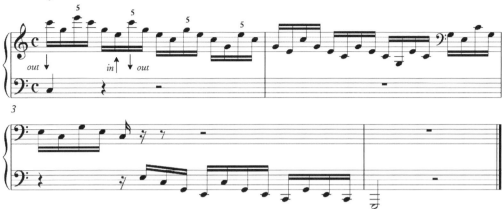

Example 13. Beethoven Concerto Op. 15. Another Way to Shape ♪.

What if Beethoven had written his concerto in example 13 in the key of C-sharp? The hand would have to be placed *in* to accommodate the short fingers, one and five, when they are required to play on the short keys. When the thumb plays E-sharp (white), it should play near the entrance to the black keys, just next to the F-sharp, allowing 5 to begin the group from a little out, more toward the outer edge of the black key. The general feeling is a shaping movement *in* toward the thumb from 5, which is a little out. Note that the left hand moves *in* to 5 and thumb before moving slightly out in order to move back in again toward 5. (Yes, it is more efficient to move—in this case, to shape—than it is to lock the hand in a position that blocks the chord. In blocking chords, the fingers become isolated from the hand and forearm, limiting freedom and reducing brilliance. But this is a separate topic.)

Example 14. Beethoven Concerto Op. 15. On C-Sharp Major ♪.

The Shape

I point out the obvious for a reason. The position of the hand in relation to the black keys is not always decided for us as in the examples cited above. More often than not, the score requires us to move between the two locations.

And here, as they say, is where the rubber hits the road, or in our parlance, where the finger meets the key.

Legend has it that Chopin liked to teach B major as an introductory scale. The dizzying number of sharps aside, this makes very good sense because it shows the student a comfortable, natural position for the hand: long fingers on short keys and short fingers on long keys. Chopin, of course, knew how to get everywhere on the keys, including into and out of the black keys using any finger he wanted. This concept of how and when to shape *in* and *out* is crucial to developing efficiency in speed. And this concept, in my experience, is perhaps the least understood of all, but when perfected it can have a profound result.

Example 15. B Major Scale.

Simply put, when moving in speed to a short finger on a short key, plan to be in position for that short finger, at the very latest, by the preceding note. In example 16 (♪) the shorter arrow indicates a step on the way *in* to the longer arrow, which places the 4th finger in a good position for the thumb to play on a black key without making a sudden lurch toward the fallboard. Likewise, the shorter arrow pointing *out* (high F-natural) toward the torso indicates a slight movement outward in order to go back in to the thumb on B-flat. This is called in/out shaping, otherwise known as *walking* gradually in or out. The objective is to arrive in time to play without feeling hurried.

Example 16. Chopin Ballade Op. 23. Walking In and Out ♪.

This is the passage that gave Susan pause, the one for which technical ease had escaped her and the one that, finally, with the mystery solved, felt ridiculously easy (example 16). It was one of those "aha" moments. Susan had not understood that when she depresses a key, she makes a commitment. The finger enters into a relationship with the keyboard that requires a follow-through. The position of her finger on the next key will be the direct result of her finger's position on the first key. For efficiency in speed, it is crucial that she arrive at each key without an interruption in the movement or the momentum. This requires an awareness of where her hand is on the keys, particularly relative to the black keys.

Susan turned from the piano and rummaged in her bag for another score. She pulled out her copy of Chopin Nocturnes, which fell open to a well-worn page in the D-flat Nocturne, Op. 27, No. 2. "What about this nasty figure?" Her tone seemed a challenge, but already her hands felt for the keys to apply what she had just learned.

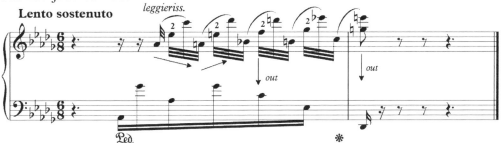

Example 17. Chopin Nocturne Op. 27, No. 2. Diagonals. Out On F ♪.

Notice that the right-hand figure in example 17 (♪) is a series of triads spanning the interval of a tenth. Because it moves up chromatically, the position of the hand changes slightly while describing diagonals as the thumb moves from black to white and back again. As the thumb moves in, the fifth finger tends to be at a slight angle out; when the thumb moves out, the fifth finger moves at a slight angle back in to the black. (Remember, as long as the fingers/hand/forearm alliance remains straight with itself, it can be at any angle with the keyboard.) Notice that when the thumb falls back the interval of a tenth (high C back to A-natural, for example), the hand moves not at an angle but laterally, in this case white to white. (Take care not to stretch for the tenth, especially if your hand is average to smallish in size. Even if you have elephant hands like Rachmaninoff, I do not recommend stretching to an extreme—ever. But this is another topic.)

Apropos of our discussion of in and out, I showed Susan that the F played by the 2nd finger moves well out. (In example 5, I placed an arrow to indicate *out*, toward the torso.) This movement in the direction of *out* facilitates the move to high D, avoiding a crash into the black keys while trying to land between those two peaks. In fact, both of the moves to fifth-finger white keys avoid similar disasters by moving slightly outward.

One more question arose regarding location. In Chopin's G Major Prelude, again the note before the thumb prepares the way for it to play *in* on a black key, as indicated by the short arrows (example 18 ♪). Notice that the thumb plays twice in a row in measure two by sliding off of the F-sharp and moving back outward slightly onto the second note, the E (indicated by a short arrow). I know. All the old wives of those ubiquitous tales are tut-tutting from beyond their graves. Incidentally, in the second half of the first measure—from

B down to F-sharp—the right hand can take over the sixteenths in order to provide a momentary relief from the continuous motion. But this is not really necessary.

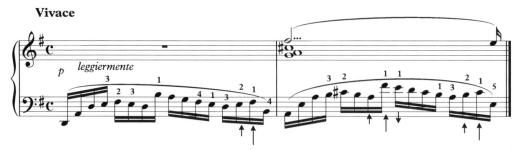

Example 18. Chopin Prelude No. 3. Preparing for the thumb ♪.

The Optimal Location

As far as I am able to determine, playing the piano has very little in common with real estate, apart from the notion that location can be everything. So, in that sense there *is* an optimal spot on which to depress the key, but that spot is not necessarily going to be at the end of the lever farthest from the fulcrum. Rather, it will be the place that provides the most direct access to a given note, a place that can be arrived at with the least effort, smoothly and without a sudden lurch. We can choose to play anywhere on the key, but in speed that "anywhere" is determined by what comes before and after.

The keyboard geography consists of plains and mountains, white keys and black keys, which to a large extent is what governs the placement of our hands on the keys. Long fingers on short keys and short fingers on long keys is a good general rule. But obviously we can play virtually anywhere in the landscape, including climbing mountains with short fingers. Shaping under (ascending right hand) and shaping over (descending right hand) can help us establish where on the keys to be relative to each other and relative to the plains and mountains. Moving in or out can help us arrive in time to play with short fingers on black keys. Avoid sudden lurches at all costs, as you might fall off a high peak or crash into the fall board.

Opportunities to implement these techniques abound in the piano repertoire; I doubt there exists a substantial piece that does not require walking in and out of the black keys at some point. In Susan's pieces there are still more refinements for her to work in, sometimes including complementary technical principles. But, if a short finger wants to play on a black key, which it has every right to do, Susan now knows to walk it there gradually in time to play and then escort it away again.

III
BOOSTING SPEED IN SCALES AND *ARPEGGIOS*

Very early in my career I played at the banana festival in Fulton, Kentucky. Yes, there is a banana festival in Fulton, Kentucky. I had been engaged by the second company of the Joffrey Ballet to play Debussy's *Images*, a ballet conceived by a distinguished Japanese choreographer. We arrived at the theater, a circus-like tent of canvas pulled taut around a center column. It was an afternoon just after a significant rain. As always when touring, my first thought was to try the piano—and to find out if there was, in fact, a piano. (I'm not kidding.) I stepped cautiously over thick cables draped casually off the makeshift riser, snaking their way to the lighting and sound center at the back of the tent. Our stage manager busied herself plotting lighting cues and ostensibly connecting the sound system for the recorded performance of Debussy's String Quartet, the other ballet on the program.

The local stage manager pointed me to stage right, behind the tent, where he said with some pride that I would find the Steinway. Sure enough, there it was, standing alone and glistening with droplets of rain from the passing storm. My heart leapt up as I tried to process the information before me: a Steinway left out in the rain. When I agreed to play *Images,* the first piece of which is "Reflets dans l'eau" ("Reflections in the Water"), I hadn't realized it would be literal. This had the earmarks of a performance-art piece.

The piano top had been down. Still, as my fingers negotiated the scalar twists and turns of Debussy's light darting through riplets of water, I felt a heavy unevenness in the action, and the sound was dull, nothing like the sparkle Debussy had in mind. The piano felt soggy.

Yes, there is a point to this story and here it is. Despite my training, my first instinct was to work harder to get the sound I wanted, to go deeper into the key to force evenness in the action. But reason came to my rescue; technique won the day. I realized that it would not help to change my technique at the last minute to try, probably futilely, to accommodate a defective instrument. Digging deeper into the key would only tie me in knots and slow me down, something the dancers would certainly not appreciate.

To complicate matters even more, our stage manager spent too much time programming lighting cues, leaving the sound system to the last minute. It was an hour before curtain when word came backstage that there would be no sound system, and would I please play the Debussy String Quartet on the piano? I had played it once in rehearsal, so it wasn't completely new to me. But again, in a pinch it is better to ignore the voices of panic and proceed calmly forward in clarity. Knowledge always wins the day.

Still early in my career, but some time later, I had the great pleasure of working with a soprano with a voice of spun silk. She could float a high pianissimo until your heart shattered into smithereens. As part of our contractual agreement one concert season, we were obliged to present in the public schools something called an *informance*. This consisted of some performing and some talking, mostly about the process of preparing for performance. I referred to these occasions as glimpses into the artist's workshop, just to shave a bit of anxiety off the edges—we had to perform at 9:00 in the morning.

After one such *informance*, during which Janet sang her high pianissimos perfectly and had the junior-high students in the palm of her hand, I complimented her on the beauty of sound and expressivity in her delivery. She looked me directly in the face, crossed her eyes slightly and said, "Honey, at this hour of the morning that was sheer technique." She meant, I think, that by focusing on how she produced the sound, she was able to transcend other distractions. Once again, technique wins the day.

When I first started piano as a child, no one mentioned the word *technique* to me, at least not that I recall. This is probably both a good thing and a bad thing. On the one hand, I showed an aptitude for facile playing early on. But, of course, I had no idea of what I was doing or how I did it. So, eventually, problems arose that gave me pause. I am grateful to my teachers that they didn't interfere with what I could do naturally. But, oh how I wish there had been someone to show me the how-tos and wherefores of those bits that had me mystified.

It seems reasonable to assume that a child's early training includes concepts that will later have to be unlearned. For example, it is extremely important to learn note values: A whole note must be held down for all of its four counts. It is also important to get the hand onto the keys: Every little finger lives in its own little house. Neither of these concepts is true. A whole note does indeed have a rhythmic value of four counts, but in many—perhaps most—cases it does not have to be held down, at least not when playing concert repertoire. The living arrangement of the fingers was designed to get all of the fingers into a certain position on the keys, a position that will later prove, more often than not, inefficient. The fingers are in fact itinerant and the thumb is virtually homeless. When velocity seems unattainable, then, it is very likely the result of some long-standing misunderstanding of what is required of the playing mechanism, the finger-hand-arm alliance.

A student asks about boosting speed in the study of scales and *arpeggios* as they appear in repertoire. As always, my advice is to play no slower than needed and not faster than you can, meaning that at each tempo, from slow to fast, the technique always feels easy.

This begs the question, how does one achieve ease? Well, the first step is to solve the physical problem(s), decide what is needed for speed and work that in slowly. Yes, this is possible with knowledge of how the playing mechanism works. (See *Piano Technique Demystified: Insights into Problem Solving*.)

Here are some questions to ask yourself: What fingering will allow me to group notes to keep them under my hand without extreme stretches? How do I use the last note of one group to get to the first note of the next group? Is there a shape to the passage, under or over, in or out? What is the angle of my forearm relative to the keyboard, meaning, if I am approaching a thumb crossing, do I have my thumb more or less behind each finger as it plays on the way to the thumb? Working up to top tempo is an excellent use of the metronome, especially when working in sections. I do not recommend using the metronome for playing through an entire work.

Another student writes:

> Is there a most efficient approach to achieving speed? Unevenness in runs and mistakes in tricky passages often seem to result from inhibitory muscle tension (the readiness to stop a motion that is wrong). When playing music I can often *feel* mistakes or complete disasters coming seconds before they occur. This may be a slow tightening of the don't-do-that muscles.

His main question is about achieving speed and accuracy in scales and passages. From what he describes, though, I get the impression—this is impossible to know without watching him play—that he is not at rest at the bottom of the key. That is, he seems to be holding ("inhibitory muscle tension"), instead of releasing. I suggested he try this on one note: Drop into the key with a finger/hand/forearm aligned in such a way that it feels like a single unit, not pressing down past the key bed and not lifting up. He needs to find out what it takes to stand there; he is not tense, neither is he relaxed. This is akin to standing at ease, as in the army, or sitting passively in a chair. The next step is to find out how to transfer that weight to the next note via forearm rotation.

If you "cannot play a particular pattern," you haven't found the technical solution(s). I know this sounds like a cop out, but there are always answers. When playing scales and *arpeggios*, for example, make sure that the thumb is approximately behind the finger playing as you approach the crossing (example 19 ♪). They have similar shapes that are crucial for efficiency in speed, the chief difference being that in an *arpeggio* the arm is slightly more extended at the thumb crossing. Look at the scale below. The forearm is level, no break in the wrist, as the thumb begins. This is the lowest point. The forearm assists in bringing the hand up by raising *slightly for* the 2nd finger and *slightly* more for the 3rd finger. (You still play down into the key; the piano is always down.) Approaching the thumb, notice that your forearm will be at an angle with the keyboard in order to allow the thumb to play rotationally, also down, as it passes under with minimum flexion. Continue up with 3, down with 4 and 5.

Example 19. Shaping With Slight Up/Down in a Scale ♪.

19

Once the technical solutions have been worked-in, gradually increase the tempo in units. Include the thumb crossing in a unit. For example, 1,2,3,1,2 and 1,2,3,4,1,2. (See examples 20 and 21.) This is a very good use of the metronome. Play each unit at least three times at each tempo before going on to the next tempo, noting that nothing changes in the ease of playing. This repetition is not for strength training but for teaching the correct movements to the playing apparatus. When each unit feels great at the desired tempo, then try combining two units and working them up together from slower to faster, although you may not need to start at the slowest tempo. Don't try to work up speed until you have decided on and worked-in the technical solutions.

Example 20. Scale Shaping Practice, Under Third Finger

Example 21. Scale Shaping Practice, Under Fourth Finger.

In both scales and *arpeggios* the final result will be a gently undulating movement as the hands move laterally up and down the keyboard. The feeling at thumb crossings is smooth and continuous, with no bumps or rough edges.

We achieve speed and fluency by first understanding the particular technique required. I know, we toss around the word *technique* like throwing pasta against a wall, testing to see if it's done. I propose that we omit trial and error and work with what we know, which is that the playing mechanism will provide us all we need if we consider its design and treat it accordingly. Once we have knowledge and know how to put it to use, we can rely on it to save us when the Steinway has been left out in the rain or we have to perform at the crack of dawn.

IV
BEWARE THE MOUSE
Repetitive Use Syndrome and the Pianist

My student came for a lesson, finally, after having to cancel one because of wrist pain. "Oh, no, what have you been working on, and how could it have gone so badly," I asked. He responded, somewhat sheepishly, that he'd been under pressure to complete a recording project, and that he had had a marathon session at the computer, mousing into the wee hours. Ah, this explains a great deal. Doctors call this repetitive use syndrome; I call it foolish.

The most common repetitive motion injury is tendinitis, something that should be diagnosed by a doctor. The tendon is tissue that connects muscle to bone and because of the tremendous weight it bears, is very strong. The *itis* attached to *tendon* means there is an inflammation, usually in the shoulder, biceps or elbow, also known as tennis elbow. The injury is usually at the site of the insertion into the bone. The tendon is protected by a lubricated sheath, through which it runs. If this sheath becomes inflamed, the condition is called tenosynovitis and is almost identical to the causes and symptoms of tendinitis.

Carpal tunnel syndrome is the most common compression nerve disorder, symptoms of which include numbness, tingling and/or pain in the hand. Sometimes these symptoms are described as shocks. There might also be pain in the arm and shoulder and a feeling of weakness in the hand. There may be painful swelling in the wrist. It is often the result of a combination of factors that increase pressure on the median nerve and tendons in the carpal tunnel, rather than a problem with the nerve itself. Most likely the disorder is due to a congenital predisposition—the carpal tunnel is simply smaller in some people than in others. Work stress is another possible cause, and this is where we are here concerned.

Okay, I understand. One gets carried away with projects and forgets possible consequences—largely because the pain and discomfort usually come the next day. Griping the mouse while activating left and right clicks (isolating fingers) over a long period of time adds up to considerable stress on the playing apparatus, even when mousing on a Mac. Discomfort and pain ensue, and these are bad enough. Unfortunately, this must interrupt piano practice until the pain and discomfort subside. We can't work through pain, despite what some football coaches may advise. How can we evaluate the relative correctness in our technique if there is something already wrong in the system?

Fortunately, an understanding of how the forearm works can go a long way toward not only solving an issue at the piano, but in the case of this student, it also acted therapeutically. Rotating the forearm can feel like self massage, immediately releasing tension. We reviewed the basic mechanism of forearm rotation by gently allowing the forearm to turn on its axis in the elbow joint. If you want to try it, place you hands/arms as single units in front of you, palms facing each other. Now turn the entire unit downward toward the thumb side, as if placing them on the keyboard. Then turn back again. This can be repeated gradually faster and smaller.

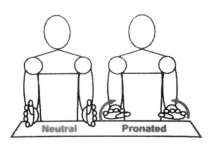

Forearm Massage

Since he reported that the pain was essentially gone and nearly all of the swelling had subsided, we decided to review basic rotation in passages from his repertoire. He worked very slowly, feeling slightly exaggerated rotation as he walked from one note to the next, transferring weight note by note. During this process, pain was forbidden.

A new student came to me recently complaining of "tightness" in his forearms and vague tingling in his fingers. A year previously he had experienced injury, but having recovered from that, he returned to practice as usual. This was not a mousing issue, but rather a case of extreme repetition, repetition of uncoordinated movements. Under pressure to complete a performance project, he felt that he may have reinstated some previous bad habits and asked me for an opinion. I have to say, watching him play, I was hard put to see any problem. His playing was fluent, his hands appeared to be operating within a reasonable range of motion. I asked him to show me passages with which he had issue, passages that seemed uncomfortable or unreliable, even if they sounded acceptable.

Here suddenly was a red flag. The piece he had been so diligently practicing contained many passages of single notes mixed in with three-note chords. The chords, interestingly, covered less than an octave as a rule, yet he felt stained. Here's why. He held his hand in a locked and open position even after striking the chords—during the playing of the single notes. Sometimes the juxtaposition of white and black keys placed his hand in a less than advantageous position, causing strain. This turned out to be mostly a grouping issue. I showed him how to group from heavier to lighter, from the chord, which gave his hand just enough respite to feel at ease (see example 2).

The moral here is to be self-aware. Take breaks from computer tasks and other repetitive activities that are potentially harmful. As we get older, and we all do, physical stress takes a greater toll than when we were young and spry, especially when we demand tasks of the body that it wasn't designed to do—like mouse-gripping for hours on end.

V
ONE HAND, TWO VOICES

We pianists have the advantage of being the entire string quartet, symphony orchestra or both soloist and *tutti* combined. Unlike single-line instruments and voices, we don't need others to complete our sonority. With this privilege comes the often awkward responsibility of organizing the various parties according to their priority. We have to make decisions about which voices to show and in what order of importance. We have to learn to do this without clinging and stretching, because those gestures are uncomfortable and inefficient. When two or more voices show up in the same hand, well, get the stretcher because there could be casualties.

Sometimes the notation is misleading. If the voice in question appears in the bass clef, must I play it with the left hand? No. If the voice has all up-stems must I play it in the right hand? No. The composer had to put the notes somewhere on the page; our job is to put them into our hands. The score shows us what the music sounds like, not how it feels physically. Consider this example:

Example 22. Beethoven Op. 13, As Written. Forearm Rotation.

It is easy to see that in example 22 the middle voice is an accompanying figure. It appears in the bass clef for notational convenience but is usually played with the right hand. The question, then, is how do we show the quarter-note melody in the treble clef and play the sixteenth-note accompaniment all in the same hand with the right voicing and even distribution? Notice that the sixteenths change direction with each note, a prime example of rotation. If you remember, in *Piano technique Demystified...* we learned that forearm rotation is how we control, among other things, the application of weight to the key; it is how we control the amount of sound. So, the first job is to feel the rotation.

But, wait. The quarters are held. Yes, so minimize the rotation, but still feel the weight shift, every so slightly, from sixteenth to sixteenth.

We still need to consider the technique of playing two independent voices in the same hand, the viola sixteenths and the violin quarters. Is it even possible to play a legato melody with this ridiculous fingering:

Example 23. Beethoven Op. 13. Melody Fingering.

Yes, and here's how:

Example 24. Beethoven Op. 13. Achieving Legato ♪.

Notice that it is the rotation from thumb accompaniment note to melody note that helps us not only technically, but musically (example 24 ♪). This rotation from the thumb, which becomes a pivot point, helps the melody feel legato because we control the amount of weight through the forearm. Take care

Example 25. Other Divisions.

not to fall on the thumb. Even though it is a starting place, it should not be accented. Judicious use of the pedal helps make connections where the same finger is repeated on melody notes.

See example 25 for some other possible divisions of labor between the hands. Measure three is particularly advantageous for smaller hands. The second beat of measure five in the melody is freer in this version.

Mendelssohn gives us a similar challenge (example 26). In his first "Song Without Words," the composer divides the viola part between left and right hands, which is quite easy when grouped in a manner similar to the Beethoven example above.

Andante con moto

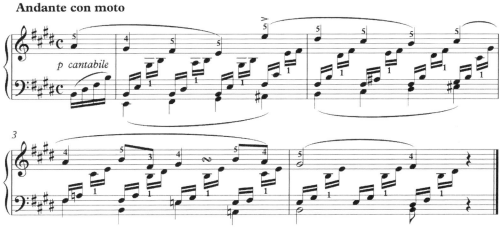

Example 26. Mendelssohn Op 19b, No. 1. As Written.

Notice that, as played (example 27 ♪), the 3rd and 4th sixteenths in the accompaniment are grouped from the thumb to the melody note. With discrete use of the pedal, the melody will give the illusion of legato. The turn in measure three is much freer if at that point the left hand takes over the accompaniment for one beat.

Example 27. Mendelssohn Op. 19b, No. 1. As Played ♪.

When working-in the technical solutions to both the Beethoven and Mendelssohn examples, notice that a slight under shape from thumb to five facilitates the movement. The wide leap in the first measure of Mendelssohn, second-finger B to fifth-finger E, is accomplished by means of a slight pluck with finger 2, which allows the hand to walk to the E. It is also possible to take the sixteenths with the left hand to avoid the leap altogether.

A student wrote to me asking about related issues in Chopin's nocturne Op. 62, No. 2 (example 28 ♪). He feels tension and a general lack of coordination when trying to manage the syncopated inner voice in relation to the melodic line. Notice the editor's fingering, making use of the principles that a shorter finger may easily cross under a longer finger and a longer finger may cross over a shorter finger. Even so, in this example there is a more coordinate way to accommodate the melody and accompaniment played in the same hand (example 29 ♪). I suspect that this student is using the editor's melodic fingering and clinging to the accompanying chords, causing unnecessary tension.

Example 28. Chopin Nocturne Op. 62, No. 2. As Written ♪.

Example 29. Chopin Nocturne Op. 62, No. 2. Right Hand As Played ♪.

Rotation is involved in the solution. But maybe the simplest way to go about solving this is to keep in mind that when playing chords mixed with single notes, the chord feels "down," slightly heavier. In example 29 (♪) you can see that I've leveled the playing field, so to speak. I think of playing constant sixteenth notes, noticing the rotation and feeling the heavier chord. One way to "feel" the heavier chord is to group from the chord, start from it. When the music changes direction with each note or chord, use single rotation; when the music is stepwise, use double rotation. The up arrows prepare the succeeding down.

I've included my fingering, but other approaches can also work. Be sure to avoid clinging and gripping, as if you were playing the organ. You can use pedal discretely. Once that is worked in, the rest is just a matter of voicing. In other words, show the melodic line relative to the accompaniment by distributing the weight accordingly. Other re-divisions between the hands are possible, but keeping the left hand free gives it a lyrical advantage.

VI
INVISIBLE POWER

I happened upon a video of Hélène Grimaud[2] playing Brahms' meaty first concerto and was reminded of Spencer Tracy's observation of Katherine Hepburn: "There ain't much meat on her, but what there is is choice." In the case of Grimaud, not only is she lovely to look at, but she is also inspiring to hear. That tiny frame produces an enormous sound and supreme virtuosity with no apparent effort. What could be the source of her power, I wonder?

Well, okay, I won't leave you hanging. If you've read *Piano Technique Demystified...*, you know that I think it takes rather little physical strength to play the piano. This is another way of saying that efficiency is more useful than exaggerated movements, efficiency being the key word. It would be more efficient to move by some natural means than it would be to stretch the hand to an extreme, which is not a natural thing to do. Even though the hand can be forced to extend, it doesn't like it because that is not in sync with its design.

This brings me to another point: What we are able to see in the technique is not necessarily the whole story. I am particularly intrigued by the title of Matthay's book, *The Visible and Invisible in Piano Technique*. Even without reading the book, much can be gleaned just from the title. It's my favorite title, I think, in the library of rhetoric on piano technique. I say this because much of what comes down to us from those proverbial old wives has to do with what can be observed in the playing of others.

I can't know what Grimaud is thinking when she plays this piece, but I can see that, although she allows her hands to open as needed, they never stay that way and they don't appear to be locked into an extreme position. But what is underneath, what invisible resource gives her so much power? If you close your eyes and listen, you might suppose that she would need to come down into the keys from some extreme height. But logic dictates that, in speed, there wouldn't be time for that. Open your eyes and notice that she is rather close to the keys. Whether the passage is lyrical and spread out beyond the octave, or whether she plays chords or crashing octaves, her hands remain more or less in contact with the keyboard.

The answer, of course, is that her power comes from discrete use of the forearm much as described by Tobias Matthay and later developed by Dorothy Taubman. She achieves speed by allowing the forearm's rotation to propel her. This natural movement of the forearm, of course, is called forearm rotation. It underlies all that we do at the keyboard, particularly in speed, and is virtually invisible. Not to put too fine a point on it, I feel the need to add that octaves or chords in speed will not succeed if the forearm is employed in an up and down, hammer-like movement. This is not an efficient movement for speed. Try it.

---

[2] Grimaud, Hélène. Brahms - Piano Concerto No. 1. www.YouTube

Even fine players sometimes report the opposite of what they do, only because they think that's what they've seen others do, or perhaps what they *think* they do. These are the so-called natural players, the Mozarts and Mendelssohns, the Horowitzs and others who arrive from the womb as fully formed pianists. They didn't really go through the how-to period of development the way mortals do.

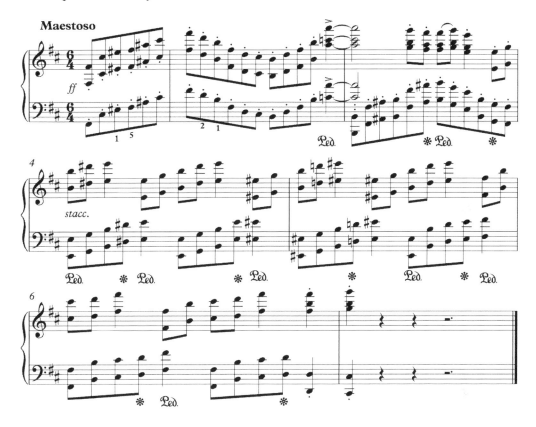

Example 30. Brahms Concerto in D Minor. Octaves As Written.

We know that octaves are played by means of a staccato technique, a plucking action and rotation (see *Piano Technique Demystified*, Chapter 23). I wonder if Brahms knew this, too. Notice that he marks the octaves with staccato dots but still adds pedal (example 30). We know that the wrist in octave playing is a little higher—but octaves are not initiated from the wrist— and that the staccato is achieved by making a slight plucking gesture with the fingers, the purpose of which is to throw the hand to its next location. But the issue is, as always, how do we do this quickly and without strain? I don't know what Ms Grimaud thinks technically when she plays this passage so brilliantly and with such power, but I can guess at what is taking place, whether she realizes it or not.

I remember from high school physics class the principle that "for every

29

action there is an equal and opposite reaction." (Who knew that something I learned in high school would actually be useful?) The action of dropping the weight of the forearm into the keys produces a reaction away from the key—if we allow it. Allowing it is crucial, and it seems to me that when we disallow this reaction by holding or tensing the forearm, this is the primary reason speed and ease of execution are inhibited. So, the downward drop into the keys propels the mechanism back up and away from the keys—passively. Through the miraculous power of our brain, we then direct the fingers to land on the next octave. To some extent the forearm controls the lateral movement, but what essentially happens is a downward attraction of gravity (passive) and a reactive thrust to the next octave (mostly passive). Piece of cake.

I know all this talk of physics can be off-putting, so let's try to put it in somewhat more practical terms. Choose a passage from example 30 and play the first octave staccato, allowing the hand to fall silently on the next octave. This is what the pluck feels like. Now add to that a very slight rotation by making a hinge of the fifth finger and the hand a gate. The gate opens to the right (right hand) and falls back onto the next octave. All quick octaves are played with one and five. No exceptions. Exaggerate these gestures slightly at first in order to teach them to the playing apparatus, but in speed they are extremely small and close to the keys. If the hand is large enough to play in an octave position along the black-key border, then do so. This will remove some in and out movements. Otherwise, plan how to shape the movement in or out from white to black or the reverse. Notice, too, which groups of notes are lateral, without movements from white to black. This will assist in shaping the passages.

Example 31. Brahms Octaves. Detail of Measure 2 of Example 18. Grouping 1.

I'm so glad I introduced the concept of groups of notes in the above paragraph. Once the octave technique is well worked-in, we still have to figure out how to coordinate the two hands. This we accomplish by deciding on which groups of octaves share a rhythmic grouping or by noticing a change of direction. We can also decide to group octaves together for the simple reason that they seem uncoordinated. This is a little bit like forging a political détente. In example 31 there is a change of direction in the left hand after the third eighth. This is one way to group this passage. Remember, though, when practicing slowly, always land silently on the next octave, thereby allowing the hand/forearm to accustom itself to being propelled to its next location. It does

30

not help to play the octave and sit on it.

Example 32 shows ways to practice grouping in this passage. Notice that when the lower note of a right-hand octave is doubled in the left, the top note can be played with the 3rd finger of the right hand, helping to facilitate.

We have learned that once the technical mechanism of staccato octaves is well worked-in, once the gesture of free-falling octaves (nearly) has been discovered, once the shapes have been decided upon and worked-in, the remaining technical gesture to consider is the vertical-ness of the passage. Where do the hands come together to begin coordinate groups of notes, and what are logical shapes? These technical groupings may or may not coincide with musical groupings, although more often than not, they are one and the same (example 32).

Example 32. Brahms Concerto. Octaves As Grouped.

But how much of this can really be observed in an operation that is based largely on sensation? When watching a fine artist perform, never does the viewer sense a struggle—it all appears so easy. That's because it is easy, and most of what is observed is the "unobservable" that supports a fine, effortless technique. Yes, really, the structural underpinning of an efficient and brilliant technique is essentially invisible.

I mention this here because of a recent experience I had with a student who came for a consultation. She had just finished an undergraduate piano major degree at an important school of music complaining of various unpleasant, if not debilitating, sensations. Her playing is secure, completely fluent and in virtually every way the playing of a young artist on her way to a rewarding career. If she hadn't presented with complaints, I would not have thought to look for inconsistencies in her physical approach. Rather, I would have sat back and enjoyed her performance.

The usual indications of a flawed technique were totally absent. Her playing was accurate and even thrilling. There were no moments of hesitation or fuzziness in passages. The tempos were appropriate and completely under control. So, what might be causing her discomfort? I know that it is not necessary to experience physical discomfort when playing the piano. In her case, though, she sometimes felt tingling, strain and wasn't always happy with the quality of the tone.

I asked her to play selected passages again. This time, on closer examination it was obvious that she extended her fingers into the air as if pointing. This was not a large gesture, but just enough to cause significant pulling away from the hand. I can hear my teacher now: "Dear," she would say, "the piano is down. The fingers only go up in order to come down again."

In other words, it is not efficient to isolate or separate the fingers from the hand individually and keep them pointing in the air, no matter how charming it may appear to the audience. When I pointed this out to her, the concept resonated and she was immediately able to incorporate a different strategy. We talked about how to apply forearm rotation to these passages.

She won't need to retrain particularly, but rather just be aware of this sensation, the sensation of being down in the key bed in order to be at "rest" and walk from note to note by transferring weight. This will reduce the strain she has experienced over a period of time and help her find the sound she wants. Remember, the quality and quantity of sound is controlled by the application of the forearm. Fingers alone cannot provide this control, no matter what you hear from those old wives.

I hope Ms Grimaud does not experience any of my student's symptoms. Because they both sound so polished, and since I know that physical excellence is largely invisible, it's difficult to know what any particular artist is feeling. But when the music works, I just go with it and assume the best.

VII
THE CASE OF THE JAZZ PIANIST
AND THE MISSING THUMB

My student brought questions about descending *arpeggiated* figures in the right hand. He is a very accomplished and much sought-after jazz pianist with considerable facility, so it was somewhat of a surprise to me that these *arpeggiated* figures were an issue. For most pianists, descending *arpeggios* are more reliable than ascending.

He has in his arsenal of licks and riffs many variants of chromatically-altered figures. These he tosses off at will as embellishments in whatever key happens to be current. This facility, it seems to me, is already remarkable. His complaint, though, was that he doesn't feel that they always sound clear and even.

I asked him to play one for me, which he did. It sounded clear and even, but I didn't tell him that at first. I asked him how it seemed to him, and he reported that it was not as clear and even as he wanted and that this has been a frustration for him for some time. After some repetitions, we found that these passages sometimes sounded uneven, too. Here we paused for a brief story.

Many years ago my teacher, John Crown, invited me to play on his live television program on public access, a program featuring new music. This was the time of direct-to-tape recording, which required playing through without the option of do-overs, adding a touch of, well let's say—added excitement. I played okay, I thought, but fluffed one descending scale-like passage. When the program aired, though, the passage in question sounded just fine. I was relieved, of course, but confused. What made me think the passage wasn't clear? It would be many years before I understood what had happened.

In a nutshell, the note(s) in question sounded but hadn't been completed. That is, the weight of my forearm wasn't supporting all of the notes equally. I wasn't transferring weight from one finger to the next as if walking from note to note. This sensation is translated in the brain as "missed" notes, because, in a way they were. The brain didn't *hear* them because the arm didn't *feel* them. Stand up. Try walking as if one ankle is sprained, not putting any weight on it. This hobbling effect is very like what happened to me on television.

Example 33. Chopin Fantasy in F Minor. Thumb Crossing ♪.

33

When we looked again at my student's *arpeggios*, we found that almost without exception, his thumb wasn't doing both its jobs, the first of which is to play the note and the second is to throw the hand into the new position. In other words, he wasn't always using—playing—the thumb as a spring board to the cross-over note as he descended. This springing action is what gives the hand the possibility of playing the thumb rotationally. I know, words fail here. Suffice it to say that rotation was missing.

As the thumb plays its note (example 33 ♪), it throws the hand over so that the fourth finger is slightly *beyond* the B-natural, which allows the fourth finger to move rotationally back into place. Exaggerate this at first, keeping in mind that in speed the gesture is greatly reduced and virtually imperceptible to the eye.

Example 34. Chopin Nocturne Op. 27, No. 2. Thumb Crossing. Rotation.

When I was a boy, I played Chopin's D-Flat nocturne (example 34) with the editor's fingering—crossing four over the thumb instead of my fingering, which is indicated above. I found his fingering difficult, to say the least, because a black-key fourth finger to white-key third finger and then second finger on the D-flat always felt too stretchy to me and never really fluent. As much as I loved playing this soulful piece, I always dreaded this passage. With the knowledge I have now, I can shape the passage with that editor's fingering and make it work. When I began to question fingerings—everything, really— and to search for ease of execution, I realized it was much more fluent to cross three to A-flat and go to thumb on D-flat, yes, a black key, and even more satisfying to cross five over thumb as the *arpeggio* continues downward. The thumb propels the hand over to five on C-flat. The moral here is that it is always more efficient to play using an easy move instead of stretching. I still prefer my fingering over that editor's. My student, though with a somewhat larger hand, prefers the editor's fingering. Go figure.

Lest I be accused of discrimination, I include here an example of *arpeggios* with the two hands together (example 35 ♪). We are aware that the hands are mirror images of each other, and therefore, when moving in the same direction, they feel as if they are doing something different. This is particularly noticeable when shaping: The right hand shapes over on the way down and the left hand shapes under. Here, though, we are considering thumb crossings. The right thumb crosses as described before, throwing the hand over to three. In the left hand it is more useful to shape slightly up to the third finger, during which time the thumb will have gradually moved in the direction of the music to a position where it can play by means of rotation. From the beginning of the *arpeggio*, the left thumb is approximately behind the finger that is playing, which gets it where it is needed in time to play.

Example 35. Brahms D Minor Concerto. Two Hands with Thumb Crossings ♪.

It took some doing, but we eventually trained his hand to use the thumb as a spring board. He had become so accustomed to playing in a disjointed fashion that it took my physically directing his hand and arm over and into the new position to make a smooth crossing. This we reviewed over several lessons, just to make sure it had been worked in and become automatic. Then, faced with the challenge of a powerful muscle memory, we applied the new technique to some of his standard licks one at a time. This is one reason why I always prefer, when retraining, to tackle new material. Eventually, though, he became more fluent.

VIII
UNCLEAR ON THE CONCEPT
Hanon and Czerny

I once served on a jury charged with deciding a slip and fall case. After listening for five days to arguments on both sides, which included much wringing of hands from the plaintiff, we decided unanimously after deliberating for ten minutes that the grocery store was not at fault. The paperwork finished and the bailiff summoned, we prepared to end our service and go about our business when one hapless juror raised his hand and said, "But I think the woman should get *something.*"

It seems to me that this is an example of that juror being unclear on the concept. If the store isn't at fault, they don't have to pay. The late, great song stylist Peggy Lee puts it wonderfully in the Lieber and Stoller song, "Some Cats Know and Some Cats Don't, And if A Cat Don' Know, He Just Don' Know." This is, of course, a great pity in the matter of civil justice. But a lack of clarity turns up everywhere, even when you least expect it.

Discussing the ideas in *Piano Technique Demystified*, a professor of piano writes: "I do believe many of the fingerings, note-grouping concepts, rotational ideas and so on make the passages easier to play than when approached with more traditional ideas." He then adds: "Many pianists' technical mastery (I know from personal experience) [parentheses his] has greatly increased after a year of vigorous Hanon and Czerny, resulting in much stronger fingers without injury."

He can't have it both ways. If rotation, grouping and shaping make the passages easier to play, why, I wonder, would he still cling to the notion that attempting to strengthen the fingers is a useful idea. My first thought was that he knows about these "many pianists" because he taught them and because that was his own path.

It's not his fault. The concept has been in the wind for generations. Due to a long tradition of misunderstanding about how to play the piano in the most efficient way, many pianists have suffered needlessly through the mindless catechism of exercises designed to "strengthen" the fingers and produce "finger independence."

I maintain that it takes very little physical strength to play the piano. In the aforementioned volume I offered as proof of this that a small child—presumably not as physically strong as an adult—can compare favorably with an adult at the piano. Most of us have observed this at one time or another. Obvious as it was to me, my argument did not hold sway with this contrary professor.

There are many references to the musculature of the fingers in the accumulated rhetoric on piano technique dating back nearly a century. Tobias Matthay discusses the use of the forearm, although in a somewhat embryonic manner, as early as 1932.[3] He writes about the 'small' (weak) and 'large' (strong) muscles. The former, called lumbricales, are situated on the inside, palmar, side of the hand, enabling us to hold a note down once sounded, but are not employed in actively depressing the key to produce sound. The strong flexing muscles are in the forearm.

From atop the pinnacle of scientific investigation, Otto Ortmann argues in favor of moderation in our range of motion: "To insist upon extreme finger-lift…is contrary to both the physiological and mechanical principles involved and is a coordination extremely difficult…to acquire. Movement is most free when the joints involved move near the middle of their ranges."[4]

Heinrich Neuhaus, celebrated teacher of Emil Gilels, Sviatislov Richter and Radu Lupu, among countless other distinguished performers of the 20th century, tells us that "the frailest, thinnest human being has all the sources of energy he needs to play the most strenuous pianistic passages as loudly as possible." He reminds us that "the piano key is only about two or three ounces. What we frequently and mistakenly call 'finger strength' is in actual fact only the ability of the fingers and hand to support any kind of load. Anyone conversant with anatomy and physiology will tell you that the strength of the fingers, properly speaking, is negligible." He goes on to say:

> I utterly disagree with the notion that muscle endurance has to be developed for playing the piano. Forcing muscles may be needed in athletics, where not only coordination but extreme strength and endurance are essential. In music, however, coordination is the name of the game; the strength that is already available in our muscles is sufficient, and we must consciously strive to conserve their sensitivity. Whatever might be gained by forcing the muscles will prove to be costly. Not only will our coordination suffer, but so will tone production.[5]

Finally, distinguished concert pianist György Sándor reminds us that the engine is located at the back of the train: "The fingers' vertical motions…are done by the antagonistic muscles of the forearm. None of these motions are done by 'finger muscles' because nothing can move itself; the muscles that do the work are always found at the adjoining component of the human apparatus."[6]

Czerny and Hanon demand that we lift our fingers in order to make them strong and independent. What if we play their exercises without lifting the fingers? In that case, whence comes the power? The forearm, of course. We can look back as far as Chopin, who felt, according to his star pupil and

[3] Matthay, Tobias. *The Visible and invisible in Pianoforte Technique.* Oxford University Press. 1932
[4] Ortmann, Otto. *The Physiological Mechanics of Piano Technique.* 1929
[5] Neuhaus, Heinrich. *The Art of Piano Playing.* 1958
[6] Sándor, György. *On Piano Playing.* G. Schirmer Books. 1995

teaching assistant Carl Mikuli, "such technical exercises are not merely mechanical, but claim the intelligence and entire will-power of the pupil…and [do] no good whatever." Of course, we pianists are free to play anything we like. But if the exercises are played correctly, that is with an understanding of the forearm's contribution, then I have to ask, why play them at all?

This professor misunderstands my argument against Hanon and Czerny and their ilk. Playing these exercises in not likely to cause injury, unless greatly misused. They are, however, not going to strengthen the fingers either. "Strong" fingers and "independent fingers" are a musical result, not a physical sensation. They are the result of an understanding of the role of the forearm. No amount of separating the fingers from the hand and arm, which is what these exercises ask for, will produce a good result. The fingers have no viable strength when separated from the hand and forearm. They work together.

Hanon A Virtuoso Pianist?

Charles-Louis Hanon was born in northern France in 1819. He studied organ with a local teacher, and we have no information as to whether he ever received advanced training. We do know that music was never his vocation. His attention seemed more focused on a monastic order. One wonders if a life of solitude somehow inspired these volumes of lonely studies he devised for piano students. They've been big sellers for nearly 200 years.

In the following examples, ask yourself which would you rather practice and why:

Example 36. C.F Hanon's *Virtuoso Pianist*, Exercise No. 1.

Or:

Example 37. Mozart K. 280.

Mr. Hanon writes that the "fourth and fifth fingers are naturally weak" and recommends practicing the following exercise (example 38). As in all of his exercises, he requires the fingers to be lifted high. (If I came across this passage in repertoire, I would use single rotation.)

Example 38. Hanon *Virtuoso Pianist*. Exercise No. 6. Fourth and Fifth Fingers.

I would rather practice shaping in this Mozart example (39) because this is how the forearm makes fingers four and five feel strong. There is nothing wrong with them; they are not weak. (See *Piano Technique Demystified*, chapter 2.)

Example 39. Mozart K. 333. Shaping for Fingers 4 and 5.

Hanon calls this exercise (example 40) "extension for fingers one and two," meaning that the right hand begins with one and two. Concepts of fingering, of course, are directly related to one's understanding of technique. This figure is ubiquitous in Classical repertoire. When I happen upon it, I play it easily, as rapidly as required and as *forte* as the passage demands by means of forearm rotation. It almost doesn't matter what fingering I choose.

Example 40. Hanon *Virtuoso Pianist*. Exercise 15.

I would rather practice single rotation in something Mozart (example 41).

Example 41. Mozart K. 333. Single Rotation.

Hanon calls this an extension exercise (example 42). I call it single rotation.

Example 42. Hanon _Virtuoso Pianist_ No. 31.

Again, I would rather play Mozart (example 43):

Example 43. Mozart K. 332. Single Rotation.

Here is an exercise that comes directly from all those old wives to whom I've often referred (example 44). The idea is that the thumb needs to learn how to pass under by locking the other fingers in place and stretching horizontally under. Nothing is said about how the thumb is to strike the key in this confined position. The thumb is never required to do this in repertoire. The tension build-up in this exercise and its companion exercise, crossing under the fourth finger, harbors potential for real discomfort. This is a complete misunderstanding of how the thumb plays (see Chapter III).

Example 44. Hanon _Virtuoso Pianist_ No. 37. Thumb Crossing.

In concert repertoire the hands very rarely double in the way that Hanon presents his exercises. I can think of some examples in Schubert piano trios and the notorious passage in the Trout Quintet. Then there's that extended passage in the Tchaikovsky Concerto. But those tend to be unusual. One might argue that, well, Hanon is saving time by training both hands at once. I would argue that time is better spent practicing the correct technical movement and not wasting time practicing something that may or may not occur in repertoire. If I understand the technical principle required, when the time comes to play showy cascades of unison doublings— in the aforementioned concerto, for example—I can then apply what I know. Playing the piano has nothing to do with building up muscles as if preparing to run a marathon. It is instead about refining physical coordination.

Czerny: Hater of Little Children?

Unlike Hanon, Carl Czerny was a serious pianist who was touted at a very early age as a prodigy. This means that with the limited musculature of a child, he was able to play on a level comparable to adults. Do you see the irony here? With the limited "strength" of a child, he was able to play as an adult. Nevertheless, he embarked on a project to devise exercises designed, he probably thought, to strengthen the fingers, though he gives little instruction on how they are to be played. He tells us to "lift the fingers high" and to "keep a quiet wrist," but we are left with the notion that success will magically occur after hours of repetitions, which I refer to as mindless rote. Play the studies as much as you want—"you can play whatever you want, dear, as long as you play it correctly," I hear my teacher say. But of course, if you know how to play them correctly, then you don't need to play them at all. You can instead spend your precious practice time solving some technical issues in music you really would like to play. By the end of his life, Czerny had produced 861 opus numbers, more than 1000 pieces for the piano. He is remembered today mostly for his vast number of exercises for piano students, exercises that are so ubiquitous that they found themselves parodied in scores by the likes of Debussy, Saint-Saens and others.

Moskowski, another great pianist who wrote piano etudes, accused Czerny of "hating little children." Indeed, within a generation of Czerny's death, his reputation as a composer had so come under fire that Brahms felt moved to come to his defense. In a letter of 1878 to Clara Schumann, Brahms wrote: "I certainly think Czerny's large pianoforte course Op. 500 is worthy of study, particularly in regard to what he says about Beethoven and the performance of his works, for he was a diligent and attentive pupil... Czerny's fingering is particularly worthy for attention. In fact I think that people today ought to have more respect for this excellent man." The reference was to an essay Czerny wrote on the correct performance of the Beethoven sonatas.

The implicit message is that through endless repetition of these studies, a pianist will somehow magically be able to play concert repertoire, that if you practice X you will be able to play Y. This is nonsense. I can't help wondering what exercises Czerny studied. The etudes he composed have been big sellers for 200 years.

I select here rather freely from Hanon and Czerny and offer alternatives, again somewhat casually, from the standard concert repertoire. The possibilities for these couplings are endless, however, and I encourage you to do likewise on your own. I suspect that part of the reason technical exercises caught on and have persisted is that they are, simply put, available. If you can reach for a pre-packaged study that purports to cover a particular technique, it exempts you from having to think for yourself and extrapolate your own examples. (See *The Pianist's Guide to Practical Technique*.) Rather than practice a study with five-finger patterns because you intend to play a concert piece with five-finger patterns—or you suppose you might someday play such a piece—go to it now and practice the patterns in context.

The first Czerny exercise in Op. 299 features the C major scale ascending and descending and fragments thereof (example 45). It is actually rather fun to play.

Example 45. Czerny Op. 299 Exercise 1.

Even so, I would still rather practice Mozart (example 46):

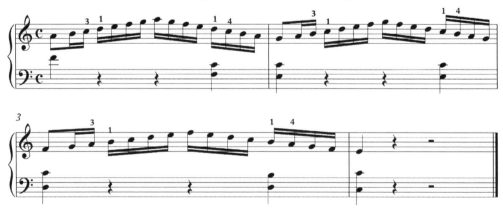

Example 46. Mozart K. 545.

Czerny offers his version of single rotation, changing direction with each note (example 47), but I find Mozart more compelling (examples 48 and 49):

Example 47. Czerny Op. 299, Exercise 11.

Example 48. Mozart K. 283. Single Rotation.

Or:

Example 49. Mozart K. 310. Single Rotation.

I've said it before and I'll say it again now: It's possible to play the piano using many different technical approaches or no particular approach at all. And

I don't care to take anything away from someone who has found something that works for him. You can find detailed information about my views on technique in *Piano Technique Demystified: Insights into Problem Solving.* I feel obliged to point out that if the afore-referenced piano professor had applied the same judiciousness to passages in repertoire that he applied to Hanon and Czerny, he very likely would have achieved the same "technical mastery," avoided mind-numbing boredom and in the process he'd have something worthwhile to play.

I once discussed these issues with a very gifted graduate student. She seemed to agree with my explanations about the relative usefulness of these exercises, or lack there of, to which she replied that she actually enjoyed playing Hanon. Well, *mazel tov*, I thought. As long as she knows why she plays them, that they are not likely to improve her technique, and if she ignores the composer's instructions to lift the fingers, then enjoy. I didn't tell her I thought playing this sort of thing as, say, a "warm-up," was really a delay tactic akin to starting the laundry, checking her email or putting on a pot of coffee before practicing.

IX
FINDING AND USING SCALES

One sunny afternoon, just as my weekly piano class drew to a close and I was racing to my studio, one of my colleagues from the local music community confronted me. We stood in the lobby of the recital hall at the university where I had just begun my tenure, I with one hand on the door. "Is it true?" she spouted, her face a puzzle of surprise and indignation. "You don't believe in scales?"

The way she framed her question with the word *believe* struck me as particularly telling. I had, in her view, committed a sacrilege. Apparently, word had spread in the piano community that I, a blasphemer, preached against the gospel and she would have none of it.

I did not think of myself as a blasphemer. Not then and not now. I am a realist, an advocate of practical use of time and energy, and my advocacy is based on knowledge and experience. But her indignation gave me pause. I knew immediately what had pressed her buttons.

At the first lessons with my students I quizzed them on scales and *arpeggios*. Did they know all the keys? Could they play all of the major and melodic minor scales hands together fluently at a moderate tempo for at least two octaves? (Notice I don't include the harmonic minor, as it is for all practical purposes what its name implies, a function of harmony and not particularly useful as we careen horizontally up and down the keyboard.) I carefully observed their use of the thumb, which in many cases was not well understood, so that became a separate technical issue. Then I blasphemed. If the scales were fluent, I would not require daily drilling, and I certainly did not want to hear them. The life of a college piano student, complex and time-challenged as it is, should not be encumbered with useless ritual. Yes, useless, time-wasting ritual.

But, Really, Are Scales Necessary?

Well, yes and no. We need to understand the topography of the keyboard and elementary keyboard harmony in order to navigate the keyboard's shoals and depths. Since we propel our hands laterally up and down the keyboard by means of certain navigational tools, of which the thumb is one, how when and where to activate the thumb has always been and remains a primary issue. So a clear feel for the relationships of white to black keys and the appropriate digits for depressing them is essential. Learn the patterns.

But do we really need to drill these learned patterns on a daily basis as, for example, in a technical exercise? Once learned and worked-in to the point of being automatic, it is no longer necessary or even desirable to repeat them in their root positions for the purpose of gaining finger "strength" or "agility" or "independence." Rarely do scales occur in music the way we learn them in exercise books. (For more on this, see *The Pianists Guide to Practical Scales and Arpeggios*.)

When is a scale not a scale? Scales serve various purposes in the music we play. They can provide melodic interest, connective tissue, embellishment or an element of brilliance for its own sake. They can direct us toward technical solutions. Our job as pianists is to notice this and organize our thinking accordingly. Here is a perfectly innocent G major scale minding its own business:

Example 50. Innocent G Major Scale.

Now add some rhythm and the innocent G major scale becomes a melody on its way somewhere:

Example 51. G-Major Scale Enroute.

Add some harmony and perhaps a touch of harp and we have a ballet by Tchaikovsky:

Andante maestoso

Example 52. Tchaikovsky's Nutcracker Ballet.

But, I hear you say, this is not really what we mean when we talk about practicing scales. True. Playing the above example from Tchaikovsky's ballet on the piano would be a technical issue of another kind. I offer it here in order to stretch the imagination, in order to plant the notion that when we encounter a scale or an *arpeggio* in a piece of music, we should be prepared to first notice that it is a scale or *arpeggio*, or part thereof, and consider it on its own terms. Does the standard fingering work here? How can we efficiently negotiate its twists and turns? I promise you the scale in your piece will not proceed innocently from G to shining G with a prescribed fingering and no detours. At least, not very often.

Can you spot the scales in example 53? Warning! This is a trick question.

Example 53. Mozart K. 281. Scales.

Easy. There's a B-flat major scale ending with a B-natural in the first measure, part of a B-flat major scale in the second half of measure two and part of an F major scale in the third measure. Right? But what about the beginning of the second measure? There are two very good reasons for noticing the scale outlined here. This rising scale-line on top has melodic interest. Yes, as we found in the Tchaikovsky ballet, a scale is a melody. Also, the technique requires us to feel a slight start on each of these top notes. What is the technique employed here, class? Yes. Single rotation, changing direction with each note. Some pianists might even go so far as to make two-note slurs here (example 54), but in my view the tempo is too fast for that.

Example 54. Mozart K. 281. Scales with Two-Note Slurs.

We see that scales can be hidden just about anywhere. Sometimes we feature them as melodies; sometimes we use them for technical facility. Or both at once. Do you see what I mean in example 55? We can show the right-hand eighths melodically and at the same time use them to help us move to each subsequent sixteenth. Do you hear the scale in the left hand?

Example 55. Mozart K. 283. Scales.

If we examine this passage further, we can find still more scales to help us play it efficiently. Notice the new groupings in the right hand of measure three in example 56 ♪, indicated by solid arrows. Just to review, we can group notes together that move in the same direction in order to facilitate their execution. These groups happen to be scales—yes I know, that's our topic. By definition, notes of a group fall more or less under the hand, leaving us with only the decision of how to get from the last note of one group to the first note of the next group. In the scale groups of measure three, we have only to move—rotationally, of course—from 3rd finger to thumb, from 4th finger to thumb and from 2nd finger to 4th finger. Not hard at all. The dotted arrows in measures two and three show how the eighth-note is plucked, sending the finger to the next sixteenth. A subtle *tenuto* on the first of each sixteenth in the left hand outlines the shape of that scale.

Example 56. Mozart K. 283. Finding and Using Scales ♪ .

Very often in quick passages it is the turn-around that can be a potential hazard. In example 57, notice the beginning of each scale and feel—not necessarily hear—a start from that note. There can be other technical principles to consider as well, but for now we want to use the scale to help us play this passage with ease.

Example 57. Mozart K. 309. Using Scales.

Bach's D Major Prelude from book one of the Well-Tempered Clavier can sound rather dull and etude-like if the pianist doesn't understand about grouping and shaping (example 58 ♪). Think of starting from each scale fragment and you will have a head start on making music. Bach's compositions are rather like essays. First he shows us what he is thinking. Then he elaborates further. Finally, at the closing he recaps what he had been explaining.

Example 58. Bach Prelude in D. WTC Book I. Scales ♪ .

Here is my favorite example of finding the hidden scale and using it to facilitate execution (example 59):

Example 59. Chopin Etude Op. 10, No. 4. Scales for Fluency.

If we follow the metric pulse, playing the sixteenth changing-note group on the pulse as notated, the passage is rather difficult. However, if we organize the passage around the scales, the groups of notes that move in the same direction (indicated with arrows), the passage is rather easy, embarrassingly so. (See *Piano Technique Demystified*, chapter 3, iDemo.)

Chopin loves to tease us in this way; it is more often than not the case in quick passage work. If a passage at first glance seems awkward and not willing to move as you would like it to, then look for hidden groups of notes, notes that fit easily under the hand. I am convinced that Chopin was very aware of these technical groupings, if only unconsciously. He was a prodigious pianist, and it is more than likely that he wrote as he played, with an automatic understanding of how the hand works. Look at these hidden scales in the Revolutionary Etude (example 60).

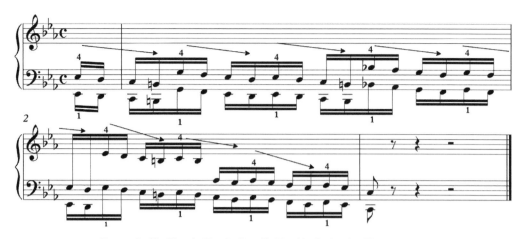

Example 60. Chopin Etude Op. 10, No. 12. Scales for Fluency.

Here is an innocent-looking C-minor scale, though oddly notated (example 61).

Example 61. Scale Hidden in Plain Sight. Right Hand.

Here is yet another oddly notated C-minor scale. Never mind that F-sharp (example 62).

Example 62. Scale Hidden in Plain Sight. Left Hand.

Can you see where I'm going with this yet? Here is another look at these two scales (example 63). Like the Tchaikovsky example from earlier, they now seem to be on their way somewhere. Notice how coyly they interact, alternating hands as if chasing one another. Taubman would leap at the chance to discuss the balletic nature of this passage. "Dear," she would say, "notice the choreography of the hands." And she would be right. In an alternating passage such as this, one hand inspires the other to play. Each hand takes its cue to act from the other, as if playing a game of tag. This is called the interdependence of the hands. We use it all the time.

Example 63. Hidden Scales. Hands Together. Choreography.

Here it is put more simply (example 64). This could be by Mozart or Beethoven. Do you recognize it yet?

Example 64. Two Hidden Scales Combined.

These innocent little scales meet up with some friends and suddenly there's a concerto by Tchaikovsky (example 65).

Example 65. Tchaikovsky Concerto. Hidden Scales And Friends.

Composers sometimes seem to deliberately obfuscate. They hide the information we need, though admittedly it is usually in plain sight. We love this about them. It makes the music interesting—exciting even, as in the Tchaikovsky Concerto—and gives us the pleasure of ferreting out all of the delicious bits. A pastry chef learns to separate egg yolks from whites, treat them each differently, then put them back together again for a light, yet rich dessert. Our ability to separate out and reassemble what we need in order to solve technical problems and make musical points is what separates artists from the casual doodler. If we learn to look for components, in this case scales and parts thereof, we cannot fail to show what needs to be shown, to voice what needs to be voiced and to articulate what needs to be articulated.

X
WHERE DO THE SMALL NOTES GO?
A Place in Time

A student wrote complaining of difficulty executing leaping *appoggiaturas* in Beethoven's Waldstein Sonata, measures 271-273 in the first movement. Remember, I said, the small notes—nuisance as they can sometimes be—become much less so when given a place in time. This concept goes for all ornaments indicated by symbols.

Here is the passage as printed in my *urtext* edition (example 66):

Example 66. Beethoven Op. 53, MM 271-273.

Notice that the small notes are printed as *appoggiaturas*, not grace notes. So the conscientious performer would logically ask, should he follow the rule and judiciously place them on the beat? Try it. This creates a small but unruly bump in the forward momentum. Now look at the suspension in the right hand. The *appoggiatura* is indeed the bass note of the chord to which the suspension resolves, albeit delayed by one note.

Example 67. Beethoven Op. 53. As Played.

What to do? Go with the momentum. In speed, the *appoggiatura* will not register as a beat anyway, so it becomes a *de facto* grace note to which is given a place in time. I play this passage as notated in example 67.

I sometimes think composers are just lazy. They give us the skeleton, so to speak, but don't always fill out the flesh. I exaggerate, of course. My complaint has to do with all of the little notes, the ones like the appoggiaturas in example 66 and the ornament in example 68 below from Schumann's *Kinderszenen*. This one is rather simple, but as you know ornaments can become very elaborate and complex. The composer gives us only the notes, leaving us to find a place in time for them—and where in the world to they fit with everything else that goes on.

Example 68. Schumann Op. 15, No. 2, A Curious Story. Ornament As Written.

Here is the way I play this one (example 69):

Example 69. Schumann Op. 15, No. 2, A Curious Story. Ornament as Played.

The distinguished harpsichordist Alice Ehlers taught the Baroque class at USC. She was a student of Wanda Landowska, who according to rumor, had been a personal friend of Bach. Irreverent students that we were, we accepted this notion without bothering to check relevant dates. I took away from that class the hard and fast rule that all trills begin on the upper auxiliary. At least in doing so, one would be more often correct than incorrect. Sources such as C.P.E. Bach, Johann Quantz, Leopold Mozart and others support this concept. It was J.N. Hummel, student of Mozart and sometime friend and competitor to Beethoven, who, in 1828, just after the latter's death, put a fly in the ointment. He declared his intention to play all trills beginning with the principal note. He justified his decision by stating it was technically easier in many instances and also smoother melodically to do so. I suspect this is the origin of much confusion today.

My practice in Classical and Baroque music—also in Chopin—is to always begin from the upper auxiliary—unless it sounds better not to.

Remember, C.P.E. Bach tells us in his *Essay On the True Art of Keyboard Playing*, after listing all the rules regarding performance practices, that if it doesn't sound good, don't do it. Sometimes I play a trill from the principal note if it is approached stepwise from either above or below. This, it seems to me, helps show the melodic line without a hiccup, without repeating the principal note. It is most important that all ornaments sound clear, unhurried and reflect the mood of their surroundings.

Consider this example from Mozart's sonata K. 333 (example 70):

Example 70. Mozart K. 333. Ornaments As Written.

Notice in example 71 that I observe the rule of *appoggiaturas*: When an *appoggiatura* precedes a dotted note, the *appoggiatura* takes the value of the note and the note gets the value of the dot (measures 2 and 3). Not all pianists do this. I think the longer *appoggiaturas* are expressive and an interesting contrast to the shorter ones—written out—in measure 4.

Example 71. Mozart K. 333. Ornaments As Played.

Of course, for our purposes here it doesn't matter which rules you decide to break or observe. It only matters that you provide the ornament with a rhythm, a place in time, and make a clear decision as to where it occurs against the other voice.

Example 72. Bach Sinfonia BWV 788. Trill As Written.

In Bach's second Sinfonia (example 72), the long trill with a second voice in the same hand, á la Beethoven's Op. 109, sometimes causes concern technically. If the tempo is no faster than 60 per dotted quarter, then play the trill in thirty-seconds; if a faster tempos is taken, then play the trill with sixteenths:

Example 73. Bach Sinfonia BWV 788. Trill As Played.

A pianist wrote to me about the trill at the opening of Chopin's Nocturne Op. 55, No. 2 (example 74). "My right-hand trilling is not consistent," he states. "I have serious trouble playing that trill without choking up. I've heard 'think about your fingers going up, rather than down' but that doesn't work. Sometimes, every now and then, I can trill effortlessly with control. But most of the time, it chokes up. I feel like I have some sort of coordination problem."

Example 74. Chopin Nocturne Op. 55, No. 2. *A* Trill. *B* As Played.

If a trill "chokes," or jams, it means that opposing muscles are both flexed at the same time. One side hasn't been allowed to release before the other side flexes. Yes, this writer has a coordination problem.

A trill sign is a symbol, and like all symbols it represents something more than itself. The most common mistake pianists make, a mistake resulting in tightness or jamming ("choking") of the trill, is conceptual. A trill must first have a place in time (example 74 *B*), a rhythm. This is true of all ornaments indicated by symbols, and they should be practiced with pulses—felt, not necessarily heard—until they become second nature. First decide on the number and rhythm of notes that will fit in the space allotted and then decide how those notes coordinate with the other hand (examples 74 *B* and 76). Remember, too, that ornaments should reflect the expressive content of their context. This example, though *forte*, is essentially lyrical, and a machine-gun trill seems inappropriate.

As a matter of technique, a trill changes direction with every note, like an *Alberti* figure. If the forearm is not allowed to rotate in its axis, albeit very slightly, the trill can jam. Cutting off the fingers/hand from the forearm is always a mistake. Do not think of lifting the fingers up and down, although they are somewhat active. Rather, maintain contact with the key, riding it (more or less) and allowing the forearm its freedom. Work the trill up slowly in rhythms, i.e. eighths, triplets, sixteenths, etc. If tightness or fatigue set in, the movement is incorrect.

Whenever someone brings Mozart's Sonata in D major, K. 311, they inevitably crash in the second movement (example 75):

Example 75. Mozart K. 311. Ornaments As Written.

It takes a bit of mind-wrapping, but ultimately this passage is quite doable:

Example 76. Mozart K. 311. Ornaments As Played.

Beethoven subjects young piano students to a trial by fire in the *Adagio* of his eighth sonata, known as the *Pathétique*. I have heard so many students approach these measures with such apprehension that the eyes glaze over and,

Example 77. Beethoven Op. 13. Ornaments As Written.

in a state of panic, the poor student throws himself at the ornaments with such determination that it sounds as if someone pushed him in the back. Never mind that the two hands seem to loose all communication with each other.

Don't let all those flags intimidate you. It's just arithmetic. Play it all in a pre-Chopin *bel canto* style, as if you have just become your favorite operatic soprano. The tempo is slow and the affect expressive; it is not a machine gun blast (example 78). And don't let anyone talk you into playing the *grupetto* in measure three on the beat. That would devalue the following thirty-second notes, creating quite a to-do.

Example 78. Beethoven op. 13. Ornaments As Played.

Chopin is undoubtedly the champion when it comes to small notes. His ornaments can be as innocent looking as a simple turn or as daunting as a splash of "17" or "22" undulating figures, all placed seemingly at random over a regular *arpeggiated* accompaniment of six notes. To complicate matters further, Chopin was, by many authoritative accounts, a classicist in the matter of ornamentation. Trills begin with the auxiliary note and should be placed on the beat. But what to do with all those grace notes, appoggiaturas and other figures loitering in the vicinity?

Example 79 is a simple case in point. Figure out the rhythm and where the hands come together. Here the quarters in the left hand support rather than obfuscate the right hand.

Example 79. Chopin Nocturne Op. 37, No. 1. Ornament As Written.

I play this passage with as unbroken a melisma as I can, taking care that it doesn't sound hurried. In my ear echoes the long-ago sigh of the most caressing *bel canto* voice I can imagine (example 80).

Example 80. Chopin Nocturne Op. 37, No. 1. Ornament As Played.

Here is a sticky example in measure five of Chopin's G Minor Nocturne, Op. 37, No. 1. Example 81 shows the original notation and, I feel obliged to add, the way many artists play it.

Example 81. Chopin Nocturne Op. 37, No. 1. Ornaments As Written.

I have always played it as indicated in example 81. Somewhere in my youth or childhood I must have read Howard Ferguson's *Keyboard Interpretation*, in which he explains Chopin's intentions. Petrie Dunn in *Ornamentation in the Works of Chopin* also gives elaborate clarifications of all of Chopin's ornaments.

Example 82. Chopin Nocturne Op. 37, No. 1. Ornaments As Played.

Chopin's *tempo rubato* consists of a steady left hand over which right hand *fioritura* frolic freely. This can cause some coordination issues if thought isn't given to the vertical alignment of the two hands. Admittedly, this seems to argue against the idea of free-flowing embellishments. Technique first; frolicking later.

Example 83. Chopin Nocturne Op. 15, No. 2 Ornament As Written.

The organization of the hands can be something like the following (example 84). Play it rather precisely at first, until the hands are well organized. Then shave off the edges until it flows smoothly and undulates curvaceously.

Example 84. Chopin Nocturne Op. 15, No. 2 Ornament As Played.

Side note: I have heard Arthur Rubinstein distort the rhythm of the second left-hand eighth (the *and* of beat one) in order to accommodate the right hand. Just saying.

The humble *arpeggio* when indicated with a symbol comes under the category of small notes. Like all ornaments indicated by symbols, it deserves a specific place in time (example 85). In Baroque music that place begins on the beat; in later music it can come before. I organize this passages and similar ones for technical ease as indicated in example 86. Start a new technical group after each of the dotted lines.

Example 85. Chopin Fantasy Op. 49. Ornaments As Written.

Example 86. Chopin Fantasy Op. 49. Ornaments As Played.

Ornamentation embellishes the main structural elements of a melody. Think of the elaborate arabesques on a wrought iron gate. Unless we figure out how to include these details with elegance and grace, they will more often than not prove to be a technical stumbling block or sound like a dilapidated pickup truck crashing into a pothole. Ornaments indicated with symbols require—deserve—a place in time. Introduce them to the other hand. I promise they'll get along just fine.

XI
GETTING THERE FROM HERE

The first time I heard the expression "you can't get there from here," I was performing at that banana festival in Fulton, Kentucky. I had asked the stage manager about getting to Washington, D.C., where I was to play later in the season, and I would be traveling from Murray, Kentucky. This memory sticks in my mind because of the shocking incident of the Steinway in the rain. Anytime I'm told I can't do something, I notice a slight bristling at the back of my neck. The same sensation occurs on behalf of students who declare they can't negotiate a particular passage.

A student brought in Chopin's soulful nocturne, Op. 27, No. 1 (example 87), the companion to the famous D-flat, No. 2, of the same opus. He observed that it is not as simple as it at first appears. Naturally, I took up my post as devil's advocate and asked that if we knew at a glance what the piece required technically, would it appear simple? This is another way of saying nothing is difficult if you know how.

My student pointed to the leaping left hand in the three-four section marked *appassionato*:

Example 87. Chopin Nocturne Op. 27, No. 1. Leaps As Written.

The first issue to consider is how to group the left-hand triplets (example 88 ♪). Instead of thinking 10ths, start each group with the thumb and continue thinking octaves in pairs. Always when leaping back and forth take care to group notes in such a way as to avoid feeling as if the arm is going in two directions. In speed this can cause a jamming of the forearm because one set of muscles hasn't time to release before the other set takes over, a condition I call lockjaw of the arm, a.k.a. lock-arm. In this example we start grouping after the low A-sharp, which takes us to the thumb by means of rotation. (Remember, the hands fall naturally and effortlessly toward the body.) Now start with the thumb and rotate to 5, allowing the hand to fall back from 5, passively, to the new thumb. In measure 5 of the example, it's possible to take that last left-hand E-flat in the right hand, although not really necessary. I understand *sostenuto* to mean a slight broadening. On the downbeat of measure 6, I take the left-hand A-flat with the right hand.

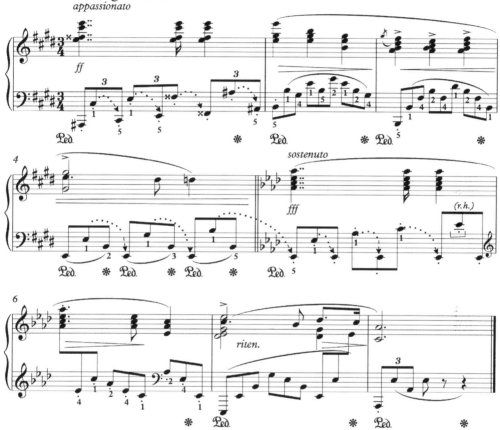

Example 88. Chopin Nocturne Op. 27, No. 1. Grouping. Leaps As Played ♪ .

But wait! There's more! My student had another question. What about the

Example 89. Chopin Nocturne Op. 27, No. 1. Leaps As Written.

63

forte section before that (example 89)? Where the *stretto* begins? This is another left-hand leaping issue.

This one is a little harder to put into words (example 90 ♪). Notice that most of each measure lies more or less under the hand, if we also shape to the wider intervals as they occur. These notes may be considered a group. The octave represents a separate voice and lies outside of the group. The technique is a combination of a leap from the octave by means of a pluck, or springing action, and a slight rotation toward the thumb.

That is, the 5th finger is like a hinge from which the 3rd finger rotates toward its landing place on the B-sharp sharp. The feeling is of 5 moving to 3. Once the hand is balanced with 3 on its note, it plays the neighboring notes in succession before opening to accommodate the ever-widening intervals played by the thumb. Take care that the hand doesn't remain in an open position (example 90).

Example 90. Chopin Nocturne Op. 27, No. 1. Leaps As Played ♪.

The last left-hand C-sharp in measure one sends the hand to the following octave by means of a pluck and a rotation. This time finger three is the hinge, which allows the hand to open to the left and rotate back to the octave. The feeling is three moving to thumb. Give the left-hand octave a little time. By that I mean go to it as if you plan to stay on it, which of course you won't. The vertical, double-pointed arrows indicate a sub grouping; feel a mini start for the left thumb along with its right-hand octave

Having thoroughly explored my student's technical issues as presented, we decided to play through the easy part, from the *larghetto* at the beginning (example 91). Normally when the objective is to consider musical issues apart from technique, I move away from the piano so as not to be tempted to watch the keyboard. This time, though, I stayed in my official teaching chair next to the piano. I was curious to see how he negotiated the opening *arpeggios* in the left hand because I knew a secret.

Larghetto

Example 91. Chopin Nocturne Op. 27, No. 1. Left Hand As Written. Editor's Fingering.

When he had finished playing the passage, I asked my usual question, "How does it feel?" He said he thought it felt "okay," which for me is a fighting word. He reported that he did not always control the sound in the left hand as he wanted. This he chalked up as par for the course, acceptable—another fighting word.

I pointed out that the editor's fingering, an attempt to achieve finger legato, creates the possibility—even the likelihood—that the hand will stay in an open position. This removes from the equation control of forearm weight, which, as we know, helps us produce and control the sound. This may have been one reason why my student felt an absence of control. I first showed him how to use the editor's fingering by means of a walking hand/arm. Then I showed him my fingering, a much easier way to keep the arm behind the finger playing at any given moment (example 92 ♪).

Larghetto

Example 92. Chopin Nocturne Op. 27, No. 1. Fingering For Control ♪.

We had already discussed the concept of moving versus stretching, so he knows it is more efficient to move than to stretch. My fingering helps to keep the hand relatively closed, a position my hand thanks me for. The concept here is that the hand casually covers mostly an octave position, though not locked,

Larghetto

Example 93. Chopin Nocturne Op. 27, No. 1. Fingering and Rotation for Control.

with occasional forays beyond. We negotiate those forays with a walking hand/arm. In so doing, we can have much greater freedom to control this opening passage (example 93) and other more gnarly ones to come (see example 94 ♪).

Example 94. Chopin Nocturne Op. 27, No. 1. Gnarly Left Hand ♪.

Here we follow the same principle of keeping the groups more or less in an octave position, but without blocking the hand in a locked formation (example 94). The brackets indicate groups of notes that fall under the hand. When the pattern moves beyond the octave, as in measure two where there are leaps of an octave and a tenth, use a walking hand/arm to assist. These are very small movements. Notice I have taken the liberty of moving the pedal markings one eighth note to the left, which keeps the lowest bass notes in the sonorities. I can't imagine Chopin wouldn't approve.

A student asks about the Chopin Ballade in G minor. "I'm having a very troublesome time with the right hand at this passage, particularly the lower octave (example 95). I don't have a problem with the higher octave part, even though they're the same notes as the lower octave. It's getting down to the lower octave and hitting the notes, particularly the A."

Example 95. Chopin Ballade Op 23. Getting There.

If the upper octave works to your satisfaction, but not the lower octave, lean your torso slightly to your left (indicated by the left arrow) as the right hand descends. This will preserve the angle of hand to keyboard. When the same passage is repeated lower, it is even more important to lean slightly to the left in order to get your torso out of the way. Remember, we can be at any angle with the keyboard as long as the playing apparatus is straight with itself. When the hand plays directly in front of the torso, there can be a tendency to twist at the wrist. The A, played with finger three, is sounded by means of a slight upward motion of the forearm (indicated by the up arrow). Very slight.

Think of the chord as the start of each group. It will be very slightly heavier. The technical concept here is that we group from the heavier to the lighter. This can have the effect, if you want, if giving a slight accent on each chord, adding syncopated interest. This last idea is an interpretive choice, a concept with which some disagree.

Finally, you state that getting there is the problem. If so, use your thumb to propel your hand over from the single D to the new lower chord. This is one use of forearm rotation. Pivot on the thumb to the left as if a string attached to the back of the hand is pulling it. Then, allow the hand to fall back to the right on the new chord. Try it rather big first, very slowly. Then make it tiny, almost invisible, as you gradually increase speed.

When faced with the necessity of getting from point A to point B, a distance not readily under the hand, consider first where the jumping off point is. Then, find the landing place. All that's left to do is decide on how to get the distance. Have the landing place in mind before moving. This is akin to checking for water before jumping off a diving board.

XII
SMALL POINT, PROFOUND RESULT

When I was eleven with nearly two years of piano under my belt, my father made a small, uncharacteristically fatherly gesture and took me with him to a rehearsal of Haydn's "Creation." A high school friend asked him to play clarinet in the orchestra, although his instrument had been in dry dock for some time. I didn't even know he had ever played clarinet. I don't know why he took me. I thank him for it, though, because, oh, the orchestra—what an exciting world I discovered that day. I went home and began composing my own "Creation," beginning with Genesis: "In the beginning…"

Later that year I entered junior high school. I noticed among the many disconcerting features of that transition from elementary school was the absence of swings and slides. What, I wondered, would we do at recess? This dilemma easily solved itself, as there was to be no recess. Instead, or rather, better yet, there was the orchestra room.

One day early in my first semester at Roosevelt Junior High I decided to approach Mr. Anderson in the orchestra room. He was busy straightening up after the beginning strings class. "I want to play the violin," I found the courage to ask. It seemed he already knew about me, though I didn't know how and as I was already a fairly anxious child, this unsettled me. "You play the piano, don't you," he asked, "and can read bass clef?" I replied that yes I could read bass clef. "Well," he shrugged as if to say 'duh,' "why don't you play bass?" It seemed so reasonable and he so kind, I agreed.

Fast forward many years to early in my senior year as a piano major in college. The bass and I had gotten on very well, and I had used it often as leverage. One morning my mother saw a notice in the Los Angeles Times announcing local auditions for Juilliard. In typical fashion, she—without looking up—tossed a remark my way to the effect that, well, what's to lose?

A full orchestral scholarship to Juilliard on double bass got me to New York, where, while completing a masters degree, I had the opportunity to play double bass under Leopold Stokowsky and Pablo Casals, record for Columbia Records—and make my New York recital debut as a pianist at Carnegie Recital Hall with a promising young German violinist. That connection led me to the Berlin Hochschule and the genesis of a concert career as a collaborative pianist.

The small gesture from my father, Mr. Anderson's insight, my mother's observation all blossomed in a way no one could predict, or even make up. This is my long way of saying that sometimes a very small point can yield profound results.

A student in the final stages of preparing the Tchaikovsky Concerto for performance pointed out certain passages that didn't feel right. He knows that such discomfort can be a red flag, so he asked, almost as an afterthought, about the following measure in the second movement scherzo:

Example 96. Tchaikovsky Concerto Scherzo. As Written.

We had already discussed several passages in the concerto that presented much larger problems, all with satisfactory solutions, making this one little measure seem inconsequential. I had noticed a slight unevenness in his performance and had already made a note to ask him about it. But he brought it up first, for which he gets a gold star.

Look at example 96 and see if you can figure out the problem. Here's a hint: It's a matter of physics. Yes, two solid objects can't occupy the same space at the same time. When the 16ths begin on the 2nd eighth, the thumb quarter-note and the attached 16ths need to be *out*, toward the torso, in order to accommodate the left hand, which is more *in* toward the fallboard. It also happens to be easier to play in that position. At the last eighth, though, the right thumb plays a black key, C-sharp, requiring the hand to move in. I asked him to play the passage for me, and I observed a sudden lurch *in* (toward the fallboard) and his wrist made a slight twist toward the thumb side. Both of these gestures are uncomfortable and unnecessary and the result was not only a bump in the technique, but in the sound as well. The solution is ridiculously simple: Move the thumb *in* in advance by shaping a little up with the third finger on the G-sharp just before the final eighth of the measure (example 97). This made all the difference, both in sound and feel of this passage.

Example 97. Tchaikovsky Concerto Scherzo. As Played.

I have noticed that on some days a theme develops all on its own, a sort of moral for the day. On the same day of the Tchaikovsky Concerto profundity another student brought in Mozart's Sonata K. 309. She played it rather confidently. When I asked her how it seemed to her, though, she at first hesitated as if it wasn't really worth the bother, then she pointed to this closing material at the end of the first-movement exposition (example 98).

Example 98. Mozart K. 309. As Written.

What was Mozart thinking? This became our initial topic. I had to admit, though I had dealt with this technical issue many times before, I hadn't really considered what the master might have been thinking. We decided to orchestrate these two bars: strings for the first two beats and woodwinds for the next two beats. We still had to figure out how to produce these orchestral choirs on the keyboard.

This is mostly a grouping and shaping issue. Really? What about all those leaps between registers? Well, I ask, how many leaps do you count? This is a trick question.

Example 99. Mozart K. 309. As Played ♪.

If you guessed one leap, you are correct. It occurs between the first and second beats of measure two, indicated by the dashed arrow (example 99 ♪). The rest of the passage flows smoothly by grouping the notes as indicated with brackets. Remember, we often group notes together that move in the same direction. Add slight under shapes to each group—particularly helpful moving from the last note of the string choir (C) to the first woodwind note (A). It's the same in the next measure.

So, dear readers, no problem is too insignificant to consider. Don't accept less than easy and fluent at the keyboard. Teach the fingers-hand-arm collaboration what it needs to know at the basest level, and it will last a lifetime.

XIII

FINGERING MAJOR SEVENTH *ARPEGGIOS*
and Other Oddities

A student wrote to me asking about fingering major seventh *arpeggios* that encompass more than one octave (example 100 ♪). He wonders if it's okay to stretch between the third and fourth fingers. What do you think, class? That's right, it is never a good idea to stretch if it feels like an extreme.

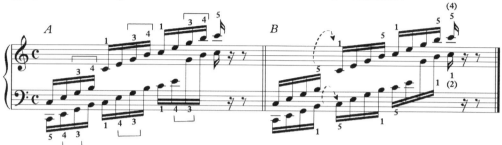

Example 100. Major Seventh Arpeggio. *A*. Student's Fingering. *B*. My Fingering ♪ .

In example 100 *A*, the brackets show where stretching can occur. If speed is not an issue, the tendency to stretch may not be a problem. It is possible to use the indicated fingering in measure *A* with appropriate shaping. But for maximum speed and fluency, I prefer the fingering in example 100 *B*. Notice that there will be a shape in the direction of *in* to play the thumb and back *out* to play 5. Remember, fluency and speed are at issue here, and these only come when the hand is at ease. If convenient in the particular passage, consider beginning with the right thumb on a different note, on E for example. This would place the left hand on E with the fifth finger.

Several examples from the repertoire come immediately to mind. In the Beethoven C-minor piano trio (example 101), other fingerings are possible, but at *prestissimo* the fingering indicated is much easier to rip off. The dashed arrow indicates a pluck and rotation from fifth-finger B-natural to fifth-finger C. The sensation is rather like rotating from five to thumb, grabbing the octave at the last second.

Example 101. Beethoven Piano Trio Op. 1, No. 3. Major Seventh *Arpeggios*.

Chopin is at his most brilliant in the F-major etude from opus 10 (example 102). I feel quite sure he would have ripped this off with the fifth finger on E as in the Beethoven example. The mechanism for achieving the crossings will be the same.

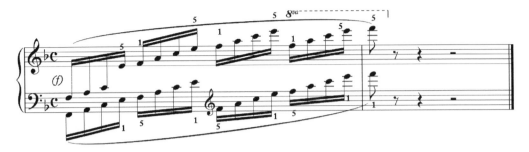

Figure 102. Chopin Etude Op. 10, No. 8. Major Seventh *Arpeggio*.

In Chopin's final prelude of opus 28, I prefer the fingering in section *A* (example 103*)*, as it has one fewer thumb crossing and feels more fluent. But *B* is also possible.

Example 103. Chopin Prelude Op. 28, No. 24. Major Seventh *Arpeggio*.

This *arpeggio* flourish near the coda of Chopin's final Ballade at first glance seems innocent enough (example 104). Give it a try, though, as written,

Example 104. Chopin Ballade Op. 52. Major Seventh Arpeggio. Editor's Fingering.

and see if it gives you a headache, not to mention finger confusion. Get comfortable with it because you have to play it twice. I tried many different incarnations before deciding on my favorite. I play it as notated in example 105. Keep in mind that the dotted 16th rhythm in the left hand is meant to match the right-hand triplets.

Example 105. Chopin Ballade Op. 52 Major Seventh *Arpeggio*. As Played. My Fingering.

And now let's look at a much simpler, albeit equally salient, issue (example 106). This is the sort of digital configuration that crops up in Classical repertoire as often as dominant and tonic. A student writes that he has trouble with a fingering turnaround featuring three, four and five. "I have trouble starting from 3, through 4 to 5 and back," he writes. "It just ruins my hand and makes it completely weak. I can play from 5 to 1 easily; I can play from 1 to 5 easily." It sounds as if he isolates his fingers from the hand/forearm collaboration when playing the turnaround with this combination of fingers. I suspect his fifth finger feels too short.

Example 106. Haydn Sonata Hob. XVI:23, Bar 25. Turnaround.

The issue he raises haunts many players. Coincidentally, this is the issue I discussed with Dorothy Taubman when I first met her. If you choose to begin the passage with 3 on the E (example 106 *A*), it is necessary to shape the passage in order to accommodate the shorter finger, 5, when it arrives at G. The fifth finger can sometimes feel like the child, who sitting on a grownup's chair, can't reach the floor with his feet. This accommodation can be achieved in two ways. (1) After 3, feel a slight under shape to 5 (notes moving in the same direction upward in the right hand often take an under shape). Then from 5, which is the lowest point, begin an over shape on the way down. This gives power to the fourth finger, as the forearm supports it. (2) From 3, which will be the highest point, gradually lower the forearm (very slightly) to 5, and back up again on the way to 3. Having said that, I use the fingering in example 106 *B*.

Another oddity that sends students running from the room in tears concerns rapid thirds—played in the same hand, so-called double thirds (example 107 ♪). I assigned Mozart's Sonata K. 309 to an undergraduate who needed an introduction to the technical concepts we've been discussing here, forgetting about the brief, yet ever so annoying double notes in the rondo. Mozart is easy for children but difficult for adults. We say this, I think, because children tend to allow their bodies to operate as designed, whereas adults tend to get in their own way. And children don't know it's difficult.

Example 107. Mozart Sonata K. 309. Double Notes ♪ .

I use the fingering in example 107, although others are possible. The dashed arrows indicate a rotation to the right, which results in a thrust into the keys toward the left. Imagine a golfer's backswing. Double notes, whether ascending or descending, are played from right to left. Allow the second finger on E in the first third to feel a slight pluck away from the key—tiny—in order to facilitate the repetition on the next third. It is the same motion when the third finger repeats C. The arrow at the end of measure two indicates a slight shape in, toward the fallboard. We remember, don't we, that the thumb likes to play in the direction of in.

Speaking of pesky thirds, a student wrote in a forum: "I have a weakness at playing thirds which I can't understand. I can descend in the right hand 5-3, 4-2, 3-1, (example 108 ♪, 2nd measure) but climbing, especially 4-2 to 5-3 (example 108, last eighth of measure one), feels totally unnatural, and my

Example 108. Beethoven Op. 81a. Thirds ♪ .

fingers feel paralyzed when I try to play at speed. I can play the rest of the movement up to speed (including bar 5 which is supposed to be much more difficult) but I can't play those rising thirds." He asks if "there is something about the technique" he might be missing. "Is there an exercise that might help?"

Yes, I respond, you are missing an understanding about the technique. No, you do not need exercises. (Someone suggested Dohnáni exercises, all copies of which should be burned in a ritual bonfire [see chapter XV]).

From your brief description it sounds as if you are trying to play the thirds as separate units, by articulating with up/down arm or hand movements or by isolating your fingers. From the B-flat and D (2-4), feel hinged on 4, release 2 and rotate slightly in the direction of the music (right). Then, rotate back to 1-3 (left) (example 108, final eighth of measure one, dotted arrow). The third finger will cross over 4, the principle being that a longer finger may easily cross over a shorter finger.

You mention that 4 and 2 to 5 and 3 feels unnatural. Again, it's likely that the rotation is missing. Feel hinged on 4, rotate to the right, turn back (leftward) to 5 and 3. This has the effect of playing the fourth finger to the third finger. Alternatively, moving from 4 and 2 to 5 and 3 can be accomplished easily by shaping slightly in the direction of *in*, toward the fallboard as you move to 5 and 3. In measure four, the brackets indicate groupings; the dotted arrows indicate the rotation. Don't be dismayed, these movements are much easier than they seem when described in words.

The descending double thirds in the Grieg Concerto, minor thirds that they are, look more formidable than they feel. The distinguished pianist Percy Grainger in his edition gives us what I think is an unnecessarily fussy fingering. Try mine (example 109). Remember, the thirds come from a rightward rotation when the hinge is on the top note; leftward when the hinge is on the bottom. (I know.) You can do it if you work the passage in slowly. It's really very, very easy. At the thumb crossings, I've placed dotted arrows. This rotation is leftward, but still turn enough back in order to feel a secure landing.

Example 109. Grieg Concerto Op. 16. Thirds.

Since we're talking about double notes, have a look at Chopin's Etude Op. 10, No. 3, the fearsome middle section (example 110). Students are attracted to the slow, lyrical opening of this wonderful piece and begin happily poking away at it in blissful ignorance—until they turn the page. Somewhere near the bottom of page two and into page three all that lyricism bursts into climactic thrusts, *con bravura*. This is why I advise students to begin a new piece at the most challenging section, which is rarely at the beginning.

Example 110. Chopin Etude Op. 10, No. 3. Double Notes.

In order to avoid feeling stretched, practice this passage releasing the notes in parentheses as if they were plucks (example 111 ♪). Use the remaining finger as a hinge, a sort of pivot. This helps the hand move to the next chord and prevents the hand from becoming locked in an open position. Feel a slight down on the first interval and up on the second.

Example 111. Chopin Etude Op. 10, No. 3. Practice Technique ♪.

Another way to practice this passage, still down and up (example 112):

Example 112. Chopin Etude Op. 10, No. 3. Another Way To practice.

An understanding of how to group notes and re-divide between the hands can help avoid stretching in this example from Beethoven's *Appassionata* sonata. Warning—the editor's fingering is not for the faint of heart, particularly the lower fingering in measure two (example 113).

Example 113. Beethoven Op. 57. Editor's Fingering.

I play this passage easily as fast as I want, lyrically and without fear of stretching or feeling otherwise uncomfortable (example 114).

Example 114. Beethoven Op. 57. My Fingering.

Further explication of example 114. Notice the hand angle in measure three:

Example 115. Beethoven Op. 57. What the Right hand Plays ♪.

Example 116. Beethoven Op. 57. What the Left hand Plays ♪.

It is not often that Mozart writes a passage of finger-twisting oddities (example 117 ♪). Here is one, though, that leaves many students scratching their heads. It is essentially a grouping problem. Remember, one principle of grouping is to organize a short note under the hand with the succeeding long note. This means planning the fingering accordingly. Focus on the moving voices and don't be afraid to let go of the tied notes (indicated with arrows). In all of the din created by the left hand ostinato, not to mention the suspensions and chromatic neighbors, those tied notes won't be missed. They will have decayed well below the dynamic level of the continuing passage.

Example 117. Mozart K. 310. Fingering ♪.

I remember tackling this Mozart sonata as a teen. Oh, the excitement, the drama, all of which I threw myself into with great abandon. Unfortunately, when I reached the infamous passage in example 117, all I had was abandon. I remember twisting and turning every which way, trying my best to cling to all of the long notes and show the moving voices somehow. If I had had the knowledge I now have, I could have saved myself much aggravation. I would have calmly examined the passage, put in a fingering—something I almost never did in those days—and let go where possible.

This is my way of reminding you—and me—that no matter what the oddity, there is a reasonable solution. If you are the way I was, you probably tend to throw yourself at a passage, making it work musically—in a manner of speaking—but not really solving all of the issues. Now we both know better.

XIV
WORKING FOR SPEED

In high school I knew a young pianist who played a very facile Mendelssohn G minor concerto, first movement. Her name was Jane. Her teacher told me that no matter how much he begged her, she wouldn't practice slowly. So, one day I asked Jane why this was, did she really only play fast all the time? Her answer was that, yes, once she knew a piece she was afraid to play it slowly for fear she would lose the ability to play fast. She may have tried it once and couldn't remember the notes.

I suspect Jane was one of those unfortunates who tend to rely too heavily on digital memory. These are the pianists who set themselves in motion and play on auto-pilot from beginning to end. They lose out on the enjoyment of beautiful details along the way and sometimes, if a finger misfires, they lose out on the notes. Slow practice is one essential part of our study, but it must be used in tandem with other concepts.

A student writes asking if I would please address the issue of speed. He is studying Chopin's prelude number three, Op. 28, and etude number two from opus 10 and can't develop the desired tempo. "In the past, many of my teachers have repeated the mantra 'speed will come'," he writes, "but I think it is silly to expect it to simply miraculously happen one day." Teachers have also told him "to practice pieces at tempo as much [as possible] but this also seems absurd. Anyone who can immediately play certain etudes at speed would be a prodigy in my book. So how do we achieve great speed without injury? How can we bring difficult pieces up to tempo?"

The one teacher is correct; speed will come, but only if the underlying mechanisms are understood. The advice to practice at tempo as much as possible lacks clarity. What should he practice at tempo? Does this teacher mean he should force the tempo ever faster without understanding first what techniques are required? Students understand that slow practice is necessary. Unfortunately, when the mechanics are not understood, he often plays differently in speed than he did at a slower tempo. Without seeing what this questioner is doing it is impossible to give a completely reliable diagnosis. However, I can generalize.

When I write about solving technical problems, I mean that we can identify solutions precisely enough to enable us to practice those solutions at a slow tempo. We figure out what we need for speed and practice that slowly, gradually working up the tempo. That's what this book is about.

In the G Major Prelude, identify groups of notes that fall more or less under the hand (indicated with brackets) and then practice that group plus one note, allowing the last note of one group to throw your hand to the first note of the next group (example 118 ♪). These are tiny movements. We can group notes together that move in the same direction. When the direction changes, the pivot note is an elision—it is the last note of one group and the first of another. Notice the job of the thumb as it rotates the hand over into the new position (indicated with *). I touch on this in *Piano Technique Demystified*. There are of course many refinements, such as shaping *in* in time to use the thumb on a black key, as indicated by the arrows (see example 18 on page 18). Shaping is, in fact, crucial to the successful realization of this piece.

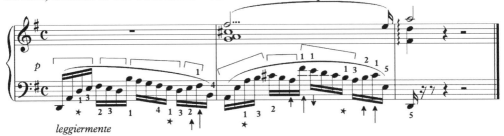

Example 118. Chopin Prelude Op. 28, No. 3. Grouping, Shaping for Speed (see example 18 ♪).

In the Etude Op. 10, No. 2, the method of working up the tempo is the same, and again only after identifying the necessary movements (example 119 ♪). In this case, the grouping is after the chord: 3, 4, 5, chord. The fingering in the Paderewski edition works, although I sometimes make adjustments. Remember, a longer finger may cross over a shorter finger (ascending) and a shorter finger may cross under a longer finger (descending). Use the chord to send your hand to the next single note; don't grip the chord. The chord is the diving board that propels your hand to the new position.

Example 119. Chopin Etude Op. 10, No. 2. Grouping For Speed ♪.

My practice plan goes like this: Once you have identified problems and solved them, write in your score the desired top tempo and a reasonable starting tempo, not slower than you really need. Then work between those two tempos in short sections, even one measure or part of a measure at a time, but always stopping on a strong beat. This is the best use of the metronome I know. Keep track of your progress in the margins. It's okay if some sections seem able to go faster than others. At this juncture, don't try to put the sections together. If a particular section won't move, if it doesn't feel easy at any of the tempos along the way, then take another look at your technical mechanisms. It may be necessary to consider additional solutions, i.e., a different fingering, shaping, grouping, etc. Never force the tempo.

Since we're still discussing practice techniques—a topic of utmost importance always and forevermore—here is a good place to insert another question. A student asks if slow practice will eliminate errors. "I want to apply [slow] practice to one piece in particular. I am having difficulty with random errors. So I have questions:"

1. Is slow practice good for eliminating random errors?
2. How slow should you go? (I have read half or quarter speed.)
3. How many repeats in a session should you do in this slow practice?
4. Should you alternate tempos within a session or over days?
5. How long would you stay doing these slow practice sessions?

Yes, random technical errors will be solved in slow practice if it is conscious slow practice. Slow practice is essential for the working-in of quick technical passages. The finger/hand/arm collaboration works best when it has the opportunity to sense clearly the movements required of it. The first step, though, is to figure out what those movements are, which, of course includes such details as the best fingering to employ.

I usually advise students to play not more slowly than they need to or faster than they can. So, take as your starting tempo one in which you feel completely comfortable—no stumbling and no hesitations. Reduce the amount of material you consider at one time. This could be as much as an entire phrase or as little as two beats. I decide, rather arbitrarily, to play the selected passage at least three times at each successive tempo, taking care that I am always focused. I am not allowed to think about what's for lunch. Each repetition should feel equally fluent. Work up each section as far as you can without feeling stressed. Then stop. If you haven't reached the desired tempo—if the passage won't go faster easily—try the same strategy again at your next practice session, keeping in mind that there may still be some underlying technical issue that hasn't been solved. Even after the passage has been satisfactorily worked up, most of my practice is under the top tempo.

This is a good way to begin your daily work on a given piece, starting with those passages that feel difficult. But once you have achieved the desired tempo (feeling easy) in all of the questionable passages, it is usually not necessary to go back to the original slow tempo, although I always practice two or three tempos slower as a review. Extremely slow practice, even in a slow movement, can also be helpful in securing memory because it removes some of the digital memory.

XV
STRETCHING EXERCISES FOR PIANISTS
The Topic That Won't Die

One contributor to a music forum for pianists offered a YouTube video of a pianist "stretching" his fingers using the keyboard as his stationary block. He worked his fingers in and out of the black keys and against the rail, claiming that these stretches made him limber. Needless to say, discussion ensued. Some wise pianists—these are the ones who agree with me—observed that such gesticulations had nothing at all to do with piano playing. If that's true, if these stretches are not about piano playing, what might they be about. I say "might" because I can only speculate. I put these "limbering" exercises in a category with other feel-good, possibly therapeutic, activities that are akin to warm-up stretches that dancers, athletes and yoga practitioners use.

I know how good stretches can feel because I do them myself—on a mat on the floor—in order to increase circulation in my limbs and wake up. I can imagine that this pianist of the video experiences similar feelings of release as he manipulates his fingers. But, no, this has nothing to do with piano playing.

The size of the hand is determined genetically. Tendons cannot be stretched. This is not to say that we can't learn to use what we have without abusing it. Speaking of abuse, one contributor shared that he derived benefit from Dohnányi exercises (example 120). Do you know the ones? The pianist is asked to hold down certain notes and lift other fingers *away* from the hand. This pianist feels he derives a "certain kind of overall limberness that's hard to describe." I suspect he can't describe it because he can't relate it to piano playing. These passages occur, let's see, *never* in the concert repertoire. But, to be fair, if they did, I wouldn't play them in the manner directed by the instigator. Dohnáni is correct when he claims no "originality or beauty" here.

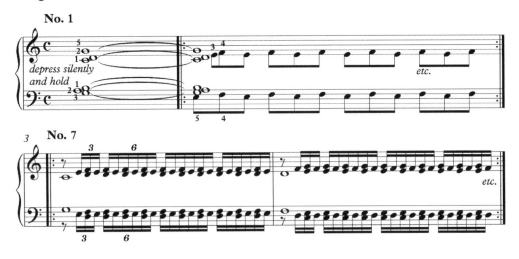

Example 120. Dohnáni's Essential Exercises For Obtaining A Sure Piano Technique.

"The exercises have to be played *forte* with all possible strength," he tells us, "slowly and with well-raised fingers, as well as *piano* in more rapid tempo." He says they are "exercises for the independence and the strengthening of the fingers." Class? Any thoughts?

Another writer felt moved to compare what pianists do with athletic training, claiming that "piano playing is above all else a motor skill." Well, I don't argue against that. But he goes on to explain that the refined motor skills we need at the piano are the *same* as what athletes use, suggesting that stretching and building strength are also part of the pianist's catechism. He could not be persuaded that athletes train large muscle groups for strength and endurance, whereas pianists train for refined physical coordination (see Chapter VIII).

A student working on Chopin's Etude Op. 10, No. 3 (example 114), asks—more than once—about stretching the hand in order to accommodate the cadenza of slurred chords. "About stretching exercises," he begins. "At the risk of belaboring the point, and one last time, what if you've done all you can to optimize hand position and you still feel strained. Wouldn't it be, under those circumstances, beneficial to have a longer stretch ability?"

Example 121. Chopin Etude Op. 10, No. 3. Stretching.

Well, yes, it might be more convenient, let's say, to have inherited from your gene pool a somewhat wider span. But as I stated above, tendons don't stretch. We have to learn to use what we have been given and move accordingly (see examples 111 and 112 in Chapter XIII). I hate to sound like a broken record, but the truth of the matter is, if your hand feels stretched—strained—then something is wrong, you haven't yet found the right movements. To be clear, the hand can be open without feeling stretched to an extreme. It is very important, though, to avoid extremes of motion. It's always more efficient to move than to stretch, even though it may sometimes seem counter intuitive. Once you feel the difference, moving rather than stretching will become the intuition.

Try this: Play each chord individually with the fingering you've decided on. How does that feel? If each chord feels fine, then the issue is not the chord itself, but how you are moving from one to the next (see example 110). You should consider where you are on the keys, probably a little more out for white keys and, of course, in for black (thumb and fifth finger). Notice if when moving from one chord on white to the next you bump up against a black key, for example. Is your fifth finger too *in* among the black keys? The problem is

Example 122. Chopin Etude Op. 10, No. 3. Reverse Slurs.

not with the passage, but rather with pianists who keep the hand too open in order to accommodate a series of chords without moving appropriately, which is the crux of the issue. Try moving the slurs over to the right by one 16th note, using the fingering in example 122. The pedal will help preserve the original articulation. This strategy works very well at allowing the smaller hand to be less open; it does, however, require some mind-wrapping.

Alicia de la Rocha, the distinguished and diminutive pianist of the Spanish persuasion, entered the forum's discussion by way of support for the idea of stretching. Someone claiming to know whereof he spoke stated that de la Rocha stretched her tiny hand so that it could reach a tenth, enabling her to play Rachmaninoff and other giants. Well, I don't know what she did. But she herself remarked once in an interview that she was blessed with a wide space between thumb and index finger and an extra-long fifth finger, enabling her to reach (she doesn't use the word *stretch*) a tenth despite having a small hand.

By now you know how I feel about unnecessary tension in the hands. You also know that, although there are many technical approaches to making music at the piano, it is possible to play virtuosically without exaggerated extensions in the hands. This latter approach I call a natural one, using the body according to its design. Stretching or pulling to extremes has no place in a fluent and efficient technique. It's the approach I prefer.

The technical sensation Lang Lang appeared in Los Angeles recently, offering up the Prokofiev 3rd concerto. He played it, apparently, with considerable flair, as expected, though Mark Swed, the Times critic, thought he seemed somehow bored with it. I didn't hear the concert, but I've heard Lang Lang on other occasions, and I can report that he is a technical phenomenon. (I can't imagine how a pianist could be bored with this piece. I have to admit, though, that once as I was sitting on a competition jury, having heard several definitive Prokofiev 3rds in a row, I decided then and there never to hear it again.)

In his review, Swed made the following observation: "His technique looked like a spectacular acrobatic embellishment of Chico's exaggerated finger work in Marx Brothers movies. That, too, may wind up a big deal. A physician in the audience quipped at intermission that he hopes the Chinese superstar has a good pension plan. Hands cannot sustain that kind of playing for long."

I rest my case.

So, don't waste time and energy and risk injury by stretching and pulling your fingers. Use them according to their design in the way that produces maximum results with the least amount of effort.

XVI
STAGEFRIGHT
Them or Us

We arrived by bus at the concert venue in a small town somewhere in Wales. I was a double bassist in the Idyllwild Festival Orchestra and one of the piano soloists on a tour of Britain. I sat about half-way back on the right side of the bus, just about to stand up, when I noticed a statuesque young woman enter dressed in a flowing gown, head held just so—she might have been playing Lady Macbeth. She made her way down the aisle with deliberation, glancing first to her right, then left, but always seeming to hone in on me. She was not one of us.

Folding herself into the seat next to me, she put one arm on the seat in front of her, leaned into me and with a mock earnest expression asked, "Do you happen to know a pianist who might be willing to play some arias with me?"

It was the Welsh operatic sensation, Gwyneth Jones—not yet Dame Gwyneth—newly in the spotlight and, although I was only dimly aware of her notoriety at the time, I was thrilled to be singled out. And yes, of course, I'll play anything.

The plan had been to feature in our concert a local pianist in a performance of Chopin's "Andante Spianato and Grande Polonaise," but the teenage pianist apparently lost her nerve when she saw the huge audience. We had already rehearsed, and she was brilliant. I felt badly for the pianist, but glad for the opportunity to appear with Miss Jones, who had agreed to provide arias with piano—with me—in place of the Chopin.

Eventually, though, the pianist warmed her feet, found her nerve and did appear. Alas, Miss Jones and I parted company, never to meet again.

In her *New Yorker* book review, "I Can't Go On," Joan Acocella gives an oh-so-right description of stage fright:

> Stagefright has been aptly described as "self-poisoning by adrenaline." In response to stress, the adrenal glands pump the hormone epinephrine (adrenaline) into the bloodstream, causing the body to shift into a state of high arousal. The person's muscles tense, he sweats and shakes, his heart pounds, his mouth goes dry, he has trouble breathing, he may become nauseated or dizzy, and his throat constricts, making his voice rise in pitch. This is the so-called "fight or flight" response, which our species is thought to have developed because it helped prepare the body for forceful action in response to a threat.[7]

The review is of a new book, *Playing Scared: A History and Memoir of Stage Fright* by Sara Solovitch (Bloomsbury). It is now on my reading list. In

---

[7] Acocello, Joan. "I Can't Go On," *The New Yorker*, August 3, 2015

the meantime, allow me to offer this one sentence synopsis right from the review: "The key thought accompanying the physical response seems to be a feeling of exposure." Exactly. When exposed, we wonder how we seem to others.

There are two possible scenarios for dealing with feelings arising from exposure, feelings we refer to as performance anxiety—otherwise known as stagefright. One scenario is that we allow the audience to draw us from the warm, brightly lit stage out to them in that vast darkness, cold and forbidding. We do this by buying in to what might be on their minds, by focusing on them. What do they think of me? Do they like me? Do I seem foolish and incompetent? This line of negative thinking also includes *I'm not good enough*, which is another way of trying to see ourselves from the audience's point of view—a point of view that is spurious at best. The audience has come to enjoy a concert and is not there to criticize or pass judgment—unless they're from the newspapers, in which case we don't really care because we know better than to read our reviews—don't we?

The other scenario is one in which we on the stage draw the audience to us by focusing on what it is we have to say. Have you ever noticed that if you stop on the sidewalk and stare up at something, other passersby will invariably stop and look to see what it is you have discovered? This focus is a powerful draw. If we can get to the point where we have prepared thoroughly enough technically and made clear choices about the meaning of the music, that is, what we want to share with the audience, then we will be able to draw them to us on the stage. When we walk out and begin to bow, our minds should already be forming the topic sentence, so to speak. What is the first idea we intend to present, and what does it feel like physically to play those notes.

This is for some performers easier said than done. It requires calm at a time when the body is gearing up for a fight or flight response. So, in preparation for walking out on stage in a state of calm focus, practice conscious breathing back stage. I once saw this in action from one of my students. Entering the backstage passage to wish my student well before her graduation recital, I found her seated in the lotus position on a blanket she had spread out on the floor. She leaned against the cinderblock wall in a state of utter repose. In front of her flickered a small candle—I thought briefly of the fire marshal—next to which were a few other items spread out as if on a picnic. She was calmer than I was. Somewhere she had learned to focus on the breath, slowly inhaling and exhaling. She knew this would slow her pulse and increase the chances of finding the right tempo at the start.

Butterflies are normal. Every performer has them. But I put this in the category of excitement at the opportunity to share something important with others who are eager to hear what I have to say. We want to be excited but not fearful. We can achieve this by focusing on the message and the means of delivery and not on the messenger or the listener.

A contributor to a pianist's forum writes: "Stage Fright! How do you deal with it? As much as I believe that getting over stagefright is a personal thing, I'm wondering how you help your students get over debilitating stage fright."

One way to zap performance anxiety is to walk out onto the stage feeling secure in your keyboard technique, knowing specifically how it is that you do what you do. Nothing is left to chance. I call this having a good conscience. This is not just about putting in enough hours; it is about using those hours to solve problems and by developing an understanding of how the body works. Have you ever stood back stage wondering if this time that passage will go well? This is the sort of thought that comes from not quite understanding how you do it. Horowitz famously reported that he didn't teach because he didn't know how he did what he did. I wonder if this is partly to blame for his own severe stagefright, resulting in a 12-year absence from the concert stage.

Fears of memory lapses can contribute to anxiety, but what may seem like a memory slip is more often than not the result of some deficiency in the technical preparations—the playing apparatus hasn't completely felt the working-in of a particular solution. Memory issues in slow passages can be the result of not quite understanding the musical point, the harmonic progression or any number of other memories that are not related to muscle memory. Butterflies never go away completely, but there is no better feeling than knowing exactly how it is that you do, physically, what you are about to do. Add to that an understanding of why you want to do it, what it is you want to communicate, and you have a winning combination.

At the moment we walk out on the stage, secure in the knowledge that we know our business, the focus at that moment should be on the first musical points—what is this passage about? What does it feel like in my hands to produce the sound I want?

Another contributor to the forum felt that the answer was insufficient, pressing the point further: "What makes some people function under stress and pressure so well, and some go to ruin, [both] on and off the stage."

Well, it seems to me this is taking the discussion to a different place. Heretofore, I assumed that the student in question felt an innate desire to perform.

There are performing personalities. These are the folks who crave the limelight, and failure is not something that crosses their minds. I know some of these, and I'm not one of them. Let's call these performing personalities "limelighters." The are at one extreme of the spectrum. There are other types of personalities at various points along this spectrum, including those who love the music, the study of it, the playing of it, but perform mostly because that seems a reasonable outcome of music study. Let's call these the "anti-limelighters." Learning to perform reliably becomes for these people a study in itself. I'm more like one of these, someone who has performed a great deal largely because in the beginning others thought I should because I was able to. This often happens to gifted children.

An anti-limelighter achieves a point of reliability in performance through an understanding of what it is that he is doing when on stage and on building a positive basis in experience. Anti-limelighters must develop their concentration skills. A person who "falls apart" probably tunes his antennae to the audience's wavelengths. He is constantly receiving, when in fact he should be sending. He should send by focusing on what is doing. This is achieved by the kind of preparation I suggested earlier. The best way to build confidence is to know how to move from one note to the next, how to play fast octaves or how to manage a large leap and why the composer writes a certain dynamic or asks us to play expressively.

True, it's harder for some than for others to organize their thoughts and focus on the task at hand. As I mentioned above, one exercise I've used is about breathing. Learn to focus only on the breath, the regularity of it, the slowness of it. Think only of breathing with regularity. In. Out.. This can help to slow the pulse and reduce the chance that tempos will be out of control.

If you suffer performance anxiety, you suffer in good company. Great performers from Cicero to Laurence Olivier, from Bette Midler to Barbara Streisand, from Vladimir Horowitz to Emanual Ax, all are on record as suffering extreme stagefright. In the end, all performers great and small have at least butterflies before a performance. We can rid ourselves of the panic, but I think without the butterflies there might be no flight.

XVII
ANATOMY AT THE PIANO

The Arched Palm

I often hear comments from teachers and pianists about the need for a pronounced "arch" in the palm of the hand. Apparently, many people sincerely believe that an arch is a necessary part of good technique, and some of these *arch-ists* are very accomplished players. They insist on the need for it.

The "arch" does not exist anatomically. If you look in an anatomy book at the drawings of the constituent parts of the hand, looking for the specific structure of the palmar arch, you will not find it. There are no bones, muscles, tendons, fascia or other membranes that make this up. Otto Ortmann explains it this way:

> To attempt to force all hands into one standard position—the normal arched position—a position, by the way, that is not even a physiological norm is seriously to restrict pianistic freedom and, in any estimation, is unwise pedagogy. It is as if we obliged each person to walk with a step of standard length, regardless of the length of the leg. The difference here is gross, but in the fine adjustments used in piano-playing even the slightest restriction is a hindrance.[8]

Let me repeat: *an arch in the palm of the hand is not necessary for the proper functioning of the hand or fingers.* Why then does this old wives' tale about the *golden arch* persist?

We know that what one sees at the keyboard sometimes can be open to interpretation. The "golden" arch, not to be confused with the hamburger franchise, is what occurs when the hand is in its unforced and naturally curved position. That's what makes it golden. When someone decides they have to *make* the hand into a curve, sometimes referred to as a tennis ball, then it becomes an arch made of *lead*. Sometimes we fall victim to misunderstanding when viewing the image of a beautifully and naturally curved hand at the keyboard and think, ah ha, that pianist must be making his hand into a curve, as if gripping a tennis ball. Gripping, forcing the hand into a curved position, requires muscles to actively pull the fingers in toward the wrist, an unnecessary and potentially tiring gesture.

The concept of the arch may have arisen in order to correct various collapses that sometimes occur in the all-important fulcra, the knuckle joints. Gripping a tennis ball, however, does not fix these collapses. And repairing collapse is a different topic.

What About the Elbow?

From a correspondent in Berlin, one of my favorite cities, comes this

---

[8] Ortmann, Otto. Op. Cit.

question: "How do you recommend the angle of the arm should be, especially on high notes? Should the elbow be close to the body or perpendicular to the keyboard, held away from the body?"

The fingers/hand/forearm alliance can be at any angle with the piano as long as it is straight with itself. The elbow shouldn't feel as if it's being held either against the torso or away from it. *Holding* implies extra tension, an unnecessary effort.

Find the position by dropping your arm straight down your side, lift up the forearm to the playing position and that should be a good location for the elbow. It hangs from the shoulder. This is not to say that it can't move outward, but take care not to involve the upper arm (bicep) excessively, as that is a slow movement. Imagine that the elbow is a hinge from which your forearm can swing from side to side, describing an arc. (Remember the circular keyboard?) If necessary, lean with the torso to the right in order to play in the upper registers.

The Role of the Forearm:
Getting to the Bottom of the Matter

A new student came to me complaining of pain and tension in his right forearm. This young man is an active performer in a rock band, though his initial training was in standard classical repertoire. I asked him to show me what he had been playing most recently when he noticed the discomfort, though of course this sort of complaint can be the result of cumulative actions. His basic position at the keyboard appeared remarkably healthy, his hands well positioned in a relatively closed position. But when he played the sort of passages he associated with discomfort, all of that changed. He locked his hand in an open position, to an extreme, and played a series of filled-in chords in an octave position, at which point I stopped him immediately.

Missing from his understanding is a basic concept of how to play rapid octaves. I doubt he gave the technique any particular thought. So, what resulted was an up and down arm movement, which is not designed for speed. Combined with this was his open hand, tensed to an extreme, especially when called upon to play a minor third between thumb and index finger. Gentle reader, if you have been following these pages you know by now that a rotation of the forearm is our quickest movement and underlies virtually all of our movements at the keyboard.

Our next step was to examine how to play successive octaves—without the filled-in chords, although it would later turn out that he had omitted a vital bit of information from the description of his performance. Octaves are played by means of a plucking action from the key (see Chapter VI), hinged at the fifth finger, which throws the hand to the next octave, a passive action facilitated by a slight rotation of the forearm back toward the thumb. I know, words usually fail without a visual aid. But this is indeed how extremely fast octaves can be managed without tension or fatigue. Because the wrist appears to be active, some pianists assume that the movement is initiated from the wrist, but it is not.

Then quite by chance in a passing remark there came the big reveal. It seems that the rest of the band left the stage drenched in perspiration due, no doubt, from jubilant gyrations at the microphones. Apparently, guitars and other instruments can be played successfully while being thrust about in high-spirited dance moves. The poor keyboard player, though, doesn't get to dance. So our pianist under discussion felt moved to get into the spirit of the music by playing with wild abandon, attacking the keyboard from high above and pressing into it in order to show—emphasis on *show*—how involved he was in the music. This, I pointed out, comes under the heading of acting, not piano technique.

The great English actor Laurence Olivier once explained to a reporter that it would be impossible for him to actually *be* Hamlet eight times a week by experiencing all of the emotions that role expresses. But by means of acting technique he could make the audience *believe* he was Hamlet. I suggested to this pianist that we focus on piano technique and then he could figure out, as needed, what he could do to add to his external display. Instead of throwing his arms at the keyboard locked and stretched, pressing and clinging to the keys, he should focus on how to achieve the sound he wanted. Pressing into the key after reaching the point of sound is useless. Remember, once the key has been depressed, only God can change it.

A student with some experience of Taubman's approach to forearm rotation wrote to me with several pertinent questions, chiefly:

> How is it possible to establish the right amount of forearm weight to be used when playing, without falling into the trap of so-called "relaxation"? I very often experience right shoulder pain, and I am not sure if this is due to a break in a fulcrum or not staying down properly on the key bottom. While we do a preparatory swing in order to play, let's say from a "C" with the 2nd finger, to a "D" with the 3rd finger, are we still balancing on the 2nd finger? When is the right moment to let the weight go from the 2nd finger and swing it to the 3rd?

I wrote back to the effect that I would need to see exactly what he was doing in order to give a secure diagnosis, and diagnosis is exactly what is needed. But I felt I could give him some things to think about.

Simply put, I wrote, you need to find out how much effort it takes to just stand on one note, feeling the connection from the tip of the finger that is playing all the way back to the elbow. Keep in mind that this unit is "like a tennis racket," as Taubman would say, though it is not rigid. The wrist is level, like a bridge between the hand and forearm. It takes some effort—though very little—and this is why the concept "to relax" is not useful. Our job in all things mechanical is to find out how much effort it takes and use only that much. You must get to the point of feeling comfortable with this balance before going on with the transfer of weight.

Try this: Practice dropping your arm into individual keys, as a unit, using one finger at a time (2-5) landing straight, upright. Stand on each finger for a few seconds and ask yourself if you feel you could stand there indefinitely—not pressing down, but not lifting up. The best analogy I can think of is that of standing upright on your feet at ease, the way I learned to do when I was in the army. The drill sergeant taught is to stand without locking the knees, crucial to being able to stand for a long period of time without fainting.

Playing the piano does not cause shoulder pain. Again, without looking at you I can't really diagnose accurately. However, first check the height of your bench; the elbow should be level with or slightly above the key bed. Then, try dropping your right arm down to your side and notice how the hand/arm unit feels. Raise it up from the elbow and rotate the hand toward the thumb side and place it on the keys, keeping that same, closed and at-ease feeling. You should now be in a perfect position to play, with all the fulcra available. It is from this position that you should explore what it feels like to stand on one note. Remember, the hand/arm unit can be at any angle with the keyboard as long as it is straight with itself. Make sure that your shoulder is not lifted in a shrugging position.

Your second question addresses the transfer of weight from one key to the next. I liken this to walking. At some point when we lift a foot and attempt to propel our bodies forward, one foot leaves the floor and all weight is on the other foot. So, just as in walking, when we swing away from one note toward another note—as in C to D with 2 to 3—at the moment 3 arrives at the bottom of the key, 2 releases, thus having transferred its weight forward. Note that if a finger strikes a key but doesn't actually feel "complete," that is, doesn't really arrive at the bottom of the key even thought it sounds, the arm registers what I call a sort of bump (see Chapter VII). This is very much like what happens if we attempt to place one foot in front of the other without transferring the weight. We call this a limp, and the result of continuous limping can be the involvement of other muscles trying to accommodate the lack of coordination. At the keyboard, this limp translates as holding, or hovering above the keys and could be a source of shoulder discomfort.

So, the simple answer to your question is yes, the weight is still on the 2nd finger until the rotation is complete and the weight transferred to the bottom of the next key.

XVIII
HANDS TOGETHER, PLEASE

I had been following a lengthy, sometimes heated, discussion on the turn-of-the-20th century practice of splitting chords between hands, sometimes referred to as rolling chords. The evidence in support of this theory is based largely, if not entirely, on recordings made at the ends of the careers of some legendary pianists who may or may not have sensed the import of these recordings. At the time, recording was a novelty, not the industry that it has become, and pianists very possibly were not thinking in terms of posterity, that they would be held up as an example of a particular style of playing. Still, there they are, these recordings, for us to ponder and marvel at. I personally love feeling the connection to the musical past.

I don't dispute the notion that chords were often rolled for expressive purposes, rolled without authorization from the composer. I do dispute the notion that composers accepted this as a given, calmly acquiescing to the casual whims of any flamboyant virtuoso who happened to strum out a tune. According to Carl Mikuli, Chopin's student and teaching assistant, "[Chopin] exacted strict simultaneous striking of the notes, an *arpeggio* being permitted only where marked by the composer himself."[9] Composers knew how to put a wavy line in the score—they often did—so why not put more of them in if that is really what they wanted to hear? It seems to me that by not putting in more wavy lines, they are telling us not to roll those chords. We have written accounts of distinguished musicians praising public performances for not deviating from the score. This tells me that, even though the practice may have been prevalent, it was not considered tasteful even at that time. It is definitely out of fashion today.

I think what we're talking about is the propensity for playing with the hands slightly askew, a sort of rolled effect, to show how meaningful the music is or how musical we are—emphasis on *show*. This was a style of playing that was both tolerated and enjoyed by different groups of players and listeners. I used to do it myself absentmindedly during the throes of adolescence to show how musical I was, not having heard anyone do it or being told to do it. It was both natural to me and annoying when I heard it back. I thought it distracted from the music. I still think so.

I'm sure some pianists in the 19th century had lazy left hands and some not. I would guess that Clara Schumann did not, as she was an advocate of the score, and to my knowledge didn't write about this or make any indications in her editions. Her student, Adelina De Lara, can be heard discussing and playing

---

[9] Mikuli, Carl. "Foreword: Chopin, Pianist and Teacher," *Nocturnes and Polonaises*, Mikuli Edition.

excerpts from Robert Schumann.[10] "Absence of affectation," she says, "was a principle of Madame Schumann's teaching." Yet, Ms De Lara can be heard breaking left-hand intervals. We know, however, from her own comments that she could barely reach an octave and would have to break chords out of necessity. She, then, would not be a model for modern day practice. Fannie Davis, on the other hand—another celebrated pupil of Madame Schumann who had a major career—rolls nearly every chord in Robert Schumann's op. 6, no. 14.[11] I've felt the temptation to do this myself in this piece, and I consider it to be a technical indulgence, a defect. Clara Schumann single-handedly changed the public concert from a circus to the more serious piano recital we know today. So, for me, she has a certain authority. It seems, ultimately, to be about taste though, which as we know changes.

It was suggested in the discussion that the modern way of playing, without rolling chords at will, began with pianists like Backhaus, Rubinstein and Arrau. Well, Backhaus studied with Eugen d'Albert and heard d'Albert play the Brahms concertos with the composer conducting. Rubinstein's education was supervised by Joseph Joachim, a close associate of Brahms. Arrau studied in Berlin with Martin Krause, a pupil of Liszt. So, I have to wonder what influenced their approaches to expressive playing. Why did they opt not to roll chords and perpetuate a style of playing that is now considered old-fashioned? I suspect they caught on to the notion that music could be still more expressive without the distraction of a rolled left hand, a superfluous ornament.

I propose that those who enjoy this way of playing do so, keeping in mind that people who know the score might think them careless. Yet, others who do not know the score might find it charming. This would be along the lines of the brilliant and eccentric pianist Glenn Gould's experiments in playing deliberately "wrong" in order to get people to listen to familiar music with fresh ears.

---

[10] De Lara, Adelina. "Clara Schumann and Her Teaching: Reminiscences and Examples." www.PianoTechniqueDemystified, Listen tab.
[11] Davies, Fanny. "Davidsbündlertänze," Op 6, No. 14. www.PianoTechniqueDemystified. Listen tab.

XIX
LEAD WITH YOUR LEFT

Muriel Kerr once told me to lead with my left. We weren't discussing ballroom dancing or boxing strategies. We were working on Chopin's D-flat Nocturne, Op. 27, No. 2, for an undergraduate performance. I didn't quite know what she meant, at least not how leading with my left would satisfy the requirements of the passage. Her advice got tucked away with "get after that," well-intentioned but not very useful instruction.

Her suggestion further complicated my as yet unformed technical expertise because I recalled her using the same remark for a completely different type of passage (example 123). In Chopin's Ballade Op. 47 the suggestion resonated. The left hand clearly provides the energy, the motor, that propels the passage forward. The main melody, however, still resides in the right hand top notes.

Example 123. Chopin Ballade Op. 47. Lead With Left.

I didn't realize at the time how to group the sixteenths and feel the vertical alignment of the chords. This would have given me all of the verve that was no doubt missing (example 124).

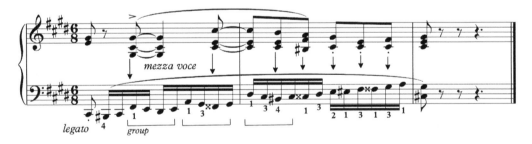

Example 124. Chopin Ballade Op. 47. Grouping.

Miss Kerr may have been trying to tell me to pay more attention to my left hand in the Nocturne. I would use the word *organize* to describe what is required. Over the years, student after student has brought in this Nocturne with only a cursory grasp of the technique. Yes, technique. In a slow piece. Technique is the method by which we accomplish anything, from bravura show piece to exquisite *pianissimo* and l*egato*.

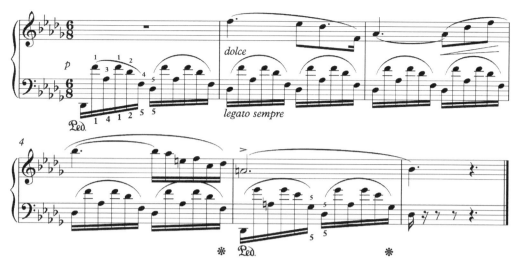

Example 125. Chopin Nocturne Op. 27, No. 2. Lead With Left. Fingering.

Sadly, I was once one of those oblivious students. I knew how the piece should sound and proceeded directly to that end. I focused on the melodic line. I pedaled haphazardly but, sensitive musician that I was, I did manage to observe the dynamics and overall phrasing. All of the good qualities I brought, though, fell victim to an arbitrary, disinterested left hand.

In example 125 I show the editor's fingering above the notes in small numbers. My fingering is underneath in larger numbers. If you've noticed similarity between this passage and the left hand of the C-sharp minor Nocturne, No. 1 from the same opus, then you are very astute. Chopin used this type of accompanying figure in nearly half of the nocturnes, by my count, and in many other pieces. My approach is to keep the hand as closed as possible in order to better control the legato, the quality of the sound, well—everything. The editor's fingering will not easily produce that result. In his fingering, the hand will be encouraged to open, perhaps more than it would like, and remain so for the entire piece.

The technique I recommend for this and all similar passages is as follows in example 126. The groups begin with the thumb, indicated by brackets. The fifth finger repeats by means of a swing and slight pluck leftward from the F followed by a rotation back to the right toward the D-flat. Try it first rather large and then make it as small as possible, barely skimming the tops of the keys as you move. Interestingly, the editor repeats the fifth finger in measure five (example 125). Perhaps he rejected that as common practice because he didn't quite understand how to do it. Just a thought.

Example 126. Chopin Nocturne Op. 27, No. 2. Leading With Left. Technique.

A student brought in the Nocturne Op. 9, No. 1, complaining of difficulty managing the melismas, all those odd groups of decorations over a regular left hand. She wasn't alone, I explained, and pointed out that, scary as it at first seems, it's really just arithmetic. But when I watched her play, I noticed that the left hand seemed rather disorganized. When I asked her about it she replied that she really hadn't given it much thought. Sigh.

Example 127. Chopin Nocturne Op. 9, No. 1. Lead With Left.

So, think we did. Notice in example 127 that again the editor wants the hand to be more open. His fingering, sparse that it is, lies over the notes in small numbers. My fingering, which is similar to the previous example, is underneath in larger numbers. The technique is as before: Use rotation in order to repeat the fifth finger. In this case, the groups begin on the low B-flats. Without this organization in the left hand, managing the ornamentation is hopeless.

Once the left hand was organized, I suggested the following relationship between the hands (example 128). Smooth out the rhythmic divisions after the coordination is well worked-in.

Example 128. Chopin Nocturne Op. 9, No. 1. Ornamentation As Played.

Later in the same piece the ornamentation is somewhat more effusive (example 129).

Example 129. Chopin Nocturne Op. 9, No. 1. Effusive Ornament.

I coordinate the hands as indicated in example 130. Don't let the eighth-note notation fool you; the scale is faster this time. (Some editions notate this in sixteenths.) Even so, play it smoothly and with grace, not like a jackhammer. As before, my fingering is in larger type.

Example 130. Chopin Nocturne Op. 9, No. 1. Effusive Ornament as Played.

Giving thought to the left hand can help us organize other types of accompanying figures (example 131). In the Nocturne Op. 9, No. 2, the left hand leaps to find a group of chords and leaps again. Take advantage of the natural tendency of the hands to fall toward the body (example 132). Practice a pluck and rotation toward the thumb side from the first low E-flat to the first chord. Use the indicated fingering to group the two chords together. Pluck the second chord and rotate back to the bass note. When practicing, take care to fall back toward the body as a result of playing the bass note, which is a sort of spring board. Land silently on the next chord group.

Example 131. Chopin Nocturne Op. 9, No. 2. Lead With Left. As Written.

Here is how I organize the technique (example 132). Use the bass notes for a passive fall rightward to the first chord. Play the chords as a group, using the second one to send the hand—pluck and rotate—back to the next bass note. The playing of the bass note sends the hand—passively—back to the next chord.

Example 132. Chopin Nocturne Op. 9, No. 2. Lead With Left. As Played.

For practice, I play the two chords and rotate to the bass note, then fall back to the right, landing silently on the following chord (example 133 ♪). The dotted arrows show the rotation down to the bass note; the solid arrows show the passive fall back toward the body. Notice the fingering. The fourth finger of the second chord rotates leftward in the direction of five, but turns back to play five in the bass. I know. Words are cumbersome. The five in the bass falls back to the second finger in the next chord. This is what it feels like. Obviously, all of the chord tones will sound. You may well ask, why not rotate from thumb to five in the bass? Try it. It feels much farther. All that's left to do is to plot where the melody and accompaniment coordinate together vertically.

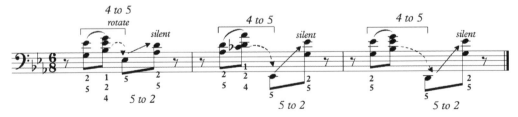

Example 133. Chopin Nocturne Op. 9, No. 2. Practice ♪.

Ballroom dancing, boxing and piano playing seem to have in common the need to think left—left foot, left hand, not to be confused with political orientation. It's understandable that in piano playing we sometimes neglect the left hand, the sinister one, because most of the melodic interest and dynamic thrust occur in our right. Most melodies, too, occur in the fifth finger of the right hand, which begs the question whether God actually intended us to play the piano at all. Assuming He did mean for us to play, let's take the position that nothing is to be taken for granted. If we practice everything on purpose, give every note its due, then our playing will be all the more satisfying as we engage in the physical process of bringing music to life.

XX
PUTTING TECHNIQUE TO USE
Emotion and Meaning

Readers of a certain age will remember the scene in "The Sound .of Music" in which Maria—not yet Von Trapp—teaches the children to sing. She begins at the beginning, a very good place to start, with the ABCs of music using the do-re-mi system. The children are remarkably precocious. Even more remarkably, in the nearby shrubbery a symphony orchestra happens to be lurking and joins the young singers. Finally, little Briggita declares that it doesn't mean anything. And she's right.

We probably agree that understanding techniques for solving the mechanics of moving laterally up and down the keyboard can make all the difference. They help us get the notes, the do-re-mis. But are there techniques, I wonder, for putting those solutions to work in the service of musical expression? Is playing with *feeling* a technique? Is playing *expressively* a technique? What if I look ever so poetic with furrowed brow and stare pleadingly at the ceiling, or bow deeply over the keys in supplication? Should I flail about at the keyboard and grasp at the air with claw-like hands?

I once played the finale from Samuel Barber's "Excursions," an exuberant barn dance. My teacher apparently thought I wasn't getting the idea of a western hoe-down and suggested I bounce around more. I tried this and felt immediately idiotic. It was perhaps the only time I openly disagreed with a teacher. Well, then, what are the expressive devices we have at our disposal for conveying to a listener that he is in fact at a barn dance? You may not believe this, but the devices are the same ones we use when playing a Chopin Nocturne or a Bach prelude: a pre-determined quality of sound infused with specific dynamics, articulation and phrasing. Yes, and we start by reading the score.

As a rule, the nearer to our own generation the score, the more information we are given. Barber gives us more than Chopin and certainly more than Bach, who requires us to study 17th and 18th century performance practices. Barber's piano pieces Op. 20 are "excursions," he tells us in his preface, "in small classical forms into regional American idioms. Their rhythmic characteristics, as well as their source in folk material and their scoring, are reminiscent of local instruments." The finale is marked *Allegro molto*. That's quite a lot of information.

But wait, as they say in advertising, there's more. In the first nine bars the outer ranges of dynamics are *forte* to *piano* with a *mezzo forte* thrown in—and don't forget the *crescendo* and *diminuendo*. There are *staccatos* and one *tenuto*. And oh, yes, there are some two-note slurs. Remember those from Baroque and Classical pieces? I wonder if this will be enough information to take the listener to the barn dance.

I'm guessing that we're close—up to the barn door, perhaps—but not inside swinging our partners allemande left and do-si-doing. I think there's a harmonica and maybe a country fiddler. Or is that a honky-tonk piano? I have to ask myself why those dynamics and articulations. How can I use them to emulate those particular instruments? If you've never been to such a gathering, have a look at Rogers and Hammerstein's "Oklahoma," the barn-raising scene featuring the iconic dance moves created by Agnes de Mille. Emulating that scene should get us inside the barn.

But what if we take a piece with a less specific program, less information? Chopin sometimes gives us a moderately provocative title, such as "Nocturne." This is about as programmatic as the composer gets. We can infer from this title that the piece will either be tranquil in nature—from the Latin root *noct*, meaning awake at night—or that the piece depicts a more elaborate scene that takes place at night, in which case it might be at times a dark and stormy one. Mikuli tells us that Chopin used the Nocturnes for teaching students "to recognize, love and produce the *legato* and [a] beautiful[ly] connected singing tone."[12] Chopin apparently taught these concepts by means of demonstration. Oh, to have been a fly on that wall.

If we look at the score, we may find more instructions (example 135). Notice at the second *Tempo I*, a recapitulation of the opening phrase, Chopin

Example 135. Chopin Nocturne Op. 9, No. 2. Expression.

[12] Mikuli, Carl. *Op. Cit*

gives us a wealth of chromatic neighboring and passing tones, embellishments on the bare bones of the tune. Tucked into these embellishments are dynamics, accents and slurs. Look closely. Why are they there? What do they mean?

We know that Chopin admired the *bel canto* style of singing, a style characterized by "rounded" tones and elaborate *fioritura* or embellishments, particularly in repetitions. Arias of Rossini, Donizetti and Bellini would most likely have been Chopin's models. Here, I think, lies the crux of our investigation into techniques for expressive piano playing.

Imagine your favorite lyric soprano vocalizing Chopin's nocturne (example 135). It would be second nature for her to rise dynamically and round the first phrase to the high G, perhaps lingering a bit—or using the consonants of the text—where the accents are. I refer to this as showing the architecture of the line, the shape it makes on the page. In the second measure she would no doubt use the rising accented minor seconds to create ever more insistent sobs on her way to an even more deliberate rounding at the high D-flat. Singers love to linger on any note above the staff. And I have to say, when done tastefully and in an appropriate musical context, this effect can be thrilling. We pianists want to be thrilling, too. In measure four she would take a little time—perhaps a lot of time, depending on her flexibility—to leap from the B-flat to the high D, where, if she had managed to place the note to her satisfaction, she would no doubt linger before sighing her way down chromatically. She would probably breathe before the final *fioritura*, which she would no doubt stretch and round off over the top, taking a bit of time. I would not expect a sensitive soprano to ever execute machine-gun ornaments in this passage a la Mozart's Queen of the Night. Of course the nature of the text would dictate her approach. (More about words later.) Do you see how Chopin has indicated these expressive touches with his notations?

Bach was stingy with expressive indications. In the entire *Well-Tempered Clavier*, Bach not only does not tell us what instrument to use, but he gives no hint of what he had in mind dynamically or in matters of articulation. It wasn't his way to give performers written instructions, though he took the trouble to write out some ornaments rather than indicate them with symbols. This was reportedly the result of a lack of faith in the virtuosi of his day, faith in their ability to realize such ornaments in good taste. He gives us only the notes, which admittedly is already quite a lot.

We have in Bach's hand a few dynamic markings for the *Italian Concerto*, the *French Overture* and the *Goldberg Variations*. These are generally uderstood to be keyboard changes on two-manual harpsichords. To the best of my knowledge, that is the extent of undisputed dynamic markings in Bach's keyboard scores. In the entire *Clavier Übung* there are virtually no articulations or phrasings indicated—at least not in the ways we've become accustomed to seeing in scores of the later 18th and 19th centuries. How, then, do we find in a Bach score what we need in order to express this music on the piano today?

Example 136. Bach C Minor Prelude from WTC I. As Written.

How threatening an *urtext* page looks (example 136). It is almost as daunting to a pianist as the white of a fresh canvas to a painter. The lack of dots, arcs and other markings, however, does not condone an absence of expression. I once attended a performance of one of Bach's large choral works in which the director encouraged his singers to give their all—non-stop from beginning to end. Afterward, a friend asked me what I thought, and I was hard pressed to find supportive comments. I mentioned something about the dynamics, and my friend proudly pointed out that they were using an *urtext* score, apparently thinking that meant they should shout their way through the entire piece, regardless of the range of moods suggested by the text. What had promised to be thrilling, I thought to myself, became rather annoying. The accompanying instrumentalists might as well have stayed home.

If we look at the example from Bach's C Minor Prelude (example 136), we probably first notice that both hands share similar figurative shapes in a sort of perpetual motion. This tendency to move constantly forward is a ubiquitous feature of Baroque music, a feature that tends to dispel drama—that is until the forward motion stops abruptly or the figuration changes, which it does later in this prelude. If you want to sound like a sewing machine, then think of this as a virtuoso display; I prefer to think of it as a harmonic passage (example 137) not unlike the preceding prelude, the C Major, from book one. I play this at about 84 to the quarter. I do this for a reason.

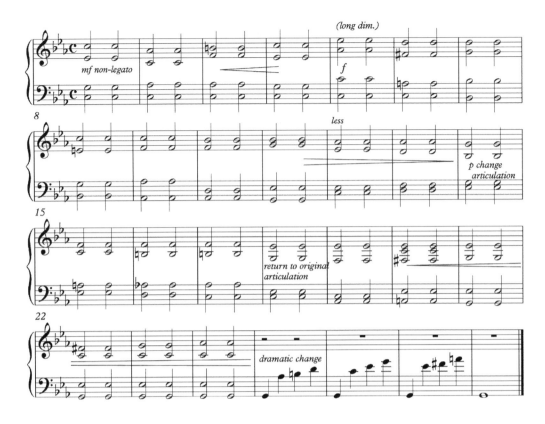

Example 137. Bach Prelude in C Minor. Harmonic Skeleton.

We play the piano. We are entitled to use the resources of the piano. We are not required to imitate the harpsichord or the clavichord. "Trying to emulate the harpsichord by leaving out natural dynamic gradations produces a motoric effect…[that] has nothing to do with 18th century musical perceptions. Baroque musicality was intensely concerned with musical shaping and nuance."[13] The notes themselves will sound like Bach, even if we swamp them with pedal—but please don't because they need air to live. If we revel in the harmonious nature of this prelude, we can enjoy not only the sonorities but use them for expressive purpose.

I begin *mezzo forte* with a nearly *legato* touch, meaning I play the figure slightly detached. Look at the architecture of the outer voices, particularly the top line, to which I give a slight emphasis. (This is why we love the piano.) The first bars introduce a long descending line from the top E-flat. One approach is to initiate a very long and gradual *diminuendo* downward. (I know, the harpsichord wouldn't be able to reproduce this, but the clavichord could—after a fashion.) Look for harmonic arrival points. For example, there is an arrival on an E-Flat sonority in measure fourteen, the relative major in root position for

---

[13] Troeger, Richard. *Playing Bach on the Keyboard: A Practical Guide*, Amadeus Press, Cambridge, 2003, p. 40.

the first time. This could be a likely place to make a change, *piano* and shorter articulation, perhaps. From here a steep climb upward in pitch and dynamic will lead us to the first dramatic change.

Just as the long line doesn't exist in Bach, at least not as we think of it in Romantic music, the short echo effect would, for the most part, also be uncharacteristic. As I stated before, a feature of Baroque music is its tendency to establish momentum, which is undermined by stopping the forward motion with a sudden shift in dynamic for repeated motifs. Now this may seem to some like sacrilege, but I also avoid terraced dynamics. On two-manual harpsichords a terraced effect may be the result when a change is made to a different keyboard, but this change is for the most part more one of quality than quantity of sound. I prefer to use the resources of the piano to imitate other sounds Bach had at his disposable: the orchestra and the human voice, either alone or in concert.

Wanda Landowska famously countered a criticism with, "You play Bach your way and I'll play him *his* way." Bach was a highly regarded performer, particularly adept at improvising, so I suspect his way was changeable. We know from the instruction he gives in the preface to the *Inventions and Sinfonias* that he preferred a *cantabile* style of keyboard playing. For more on performance practices I recommend C.P.E. Bach and Johann Joachim Quantz, who declared, "Light and shade must be constantly introduced... by the incessant interchange of loud and soft."[14]

The overarching technique for expressive playing is curiosity. We are curious to know what the composer wrote about his music and more importantly, what is the meaning of the indications he put in his score. If there are no indications in the score besides the notes, we examine the architecture of lines, the look of shapes on the page, for clues to aural shapes. We look for structural points such as cadences, even if the composer doesn't stop to enjoy them. We look for textural changes and programmatic references. In short, we look for ways to show what is different.

---

[14] Quantz, Johann Joachim. *Versuch einer Anweisung die Flöte traversiere zu spielen* [*On Playing the Flute*] (1752).

XXI
SOMETHING BORROWED
Using Words for Emotion and Meaning

I once read a concert review in the New York Post by Harriet Johnson in which she wrote that the pianist, "had fingers for the piano but no fire in his soul." The concert included, among many other works, Schubert's "Die junge Nonne" ("The Young Nun") with a noted soprano at Alice Tully Hall, Lincoln Center. The opening of the song begins with a *pianissimo* tremolo in the right hand, the left hand providing a galloping heartbeat and the clang of church bells. The conceit is a raging storm, both without and within—in nature and in the soul of the nun. The soprano enters with:

> How fiercely the storm howls among the tree-tops!
> The rafters rattle, the house trembles;
> The thunder rolls, the lightning flashes!
> And the night is as dark as the grave!

Example 138. Schubert "Die junge Nonne."

The pianist's task, of course, is to set the scene for the nun's entrance, which the composer indicates is to be whispered virtually in an undertone. I wondered if Ms Johnson read the text in the program and misunderstood what was meant to be conveyed from the stage. The words taken alone might suggest some mighty torrent of sound, complete with wind machine and cow bells. Instead, Schubert called for the opposite, a breathless, subdued excitement. He saved the torrents of sound for later on, when the nun, in a state of religious hysteria and in the key of F major betroths her eternal love to the Savior. Even then the passage is only *forte*. Oddly, when she declares that "in her heart is peace and calm," she appears to be shouting.

Did the critic misunderstand the composer's intention and blame the performers? Or did the pianist fail to convey enough *pianissimo* excitement? Both propositions are possible. For our purposes, though, let's focus on the second.

Sometimes we have in our inner ear, in our understanding, an idea so perfectly formed that it sits there demanding admiration and never makes it past the footlights. Have you ever played something for a teacher secure in the knowledge that you gave it your all, you played a real *piano* and perfect accents and other dynamics just the way they are in the score—only to be reprimanded for not doing that? Sometimes if we forget to activate our third ear, the one at the back of the hall, we can lose track of our intentions. What we mean to release from our intellect and send to the audience somehow can't find the exit and only resounds in our heads.

Or perhaps the pianist hadn't taken the trouble to study the text and relate the piano part to it. And here is where I propose that we soloists can borrow techniques from our collaborative colleagues. Collaborative pianists who work with singers know, if they're worth their salt, to squeeze every illustrative morsel from the text and incorporate it into their own part. Soloists, unblessed with words as we are, can do the same with our imaginations. In Schubert's song, the wind represented by the tremolo in the piano, is the motor that propels the drama forward. The motive in the left hand becomes the nun's opening phrase, revealing her agitated state of mind. Schubert also gives us a bell that "peals softly from the tower." With these materials we build a stage set, light it and give the drama impetus.

Example 139. Beethoven's Appassionata Finale.

With these ideas in mind, take a look at the above passage from the finale of Beethoven's Appassionata Sonata (example 139). We know that Beethoven was a man of nature. If you don't believe me listen to the sixth symphony and join the picnickers down by the river as they flee from a summer storm. Music is perhaps the most abstract of the arts. Yet, it conjures in listeners very specific emotions, emotions that often connect to individual experience, which can give rise to very specific meaning. Do you feel the gusts of wind? Can you hear the bell in the tower as it warns of impending peril?

I wonder what Chopin had in mind when he wrote this Prelude No. 14 in E-flat Minor, such a forbidding key (example 140). It reminds me of his B-flat minor sonata, the fourth movement, sometimes referred to as "the wind over the graves," coming as it does after the famous funeral march.

Example 140. Chopin Prelude No. 14.

I can hear the wind sighing through bare branches and under eaves of a darkened manse on a wild coast of Majorca (example 141).

Example 141. Chopin Prelude No. 14. Hidden Melody.

I can here state unequivocally that the pianist of Schubert's "Young Nun" steeped himself in the text and began the song with every intention of creating

110

stormy conditions, both natural and psychological. I know this because I was that pianist. Fortunately, the New York Times also reviewed the performance and gave it a rave. (Interesting, isn't it, how we can remember verbatim a negative comment and forget entirely the details of the positive?)

I consider myself fortunate to have had the opportunity to work with superlative artists in my sometime capacity as collaborative pianist. My affection for this literature began in the early 1960s in the accompanying classes of Gwendolyn Koldofsky, who instilled in her students a reverence for the text. Koldofsky had accompanied the great Lotte Lehmann, noted for her portrayals of Wagner and Strauss heroines, and particularly beloved for her strikingly intuitive interpretations of Lieder, as German art song is known.

It is from this tradition of insightful emotive skills that Koldofsky passed along to her students an appreciation of this repertoire. She showed us how Schubert virtually invented the art song as a collaborative activity, giving to the pianist considerable responsibility. When we play solo repertoire, then, we can tune into Schubert's mentality and invest in our efforts the poet's imagination. By borrowing techniques from the collaborative pianist—using our imaginations to find words or even entire scenarios—we can conjure emotion and meaning where perhaps there had been little or none.

XXII

PRACTICAL TECHNIQUE
I've Said It Before...

Given all of the negative information we have about smoking cigarettes, it startles me to see that so many people still smoke them. Likewise, given the wealth of scientific information we have today about the physiology of piano playing, I am regularly amazed at how many pianists choose to ignore it. Is it just human nature to cling to dogmas and old wives' tales of the past, to what is familiar? Could be. To me it seems unreasonable to choose deliberately unhealthy over healthy, whether we're talking about smoking cigarettes or playing the piano.

What constitutes healthy piano playing, of course, might be up for debate depending upon to whom you speak. For me it's a settled issue. I choose to play according to the design of the body. That is, I understand and make use of the physiology of the playing mechanism—a unified finger-hand-forearm collaboration—avoiding gestures that work against it, gestures such as stretching to an extreme or actions mistakenly thought to increase finger strength or independence. It is my hope that the suggestions you have just read about—hopefully, experienced—have had the effect of maximizing the efficient learning of repertoire and, concurrently, increased technical awareness regardless of your technical approach.

In the mid-1960s, Rosina Lhevinne was still the reigning empress of piano at the Juilliard School. I never had the pleasure of meeting her, this last vestige of the Russian Romantic tradition, though one frosty morning as I rushed to class, I came close to earning a place in infamy by nearly crushing the fragile octogenarian in a revolving door. A good friend studied with her and often reported to me details of her encounters with Madame. One such report made an impression, though I wouldn't know to what extent for many years. My friend wanted to play Robert Schumann's "Carnaval," and when she broached the topic with Madame Lhevinne, the response was, "Bring in Paganini next week, dear, and then we'll see." Paganini, of course, is the devilishly difficult leaping movement and would be a stumbling block for any pianist. The wisdom of Madame Lhevinne's remark reverberates all these years later and is, in a way, an underlying concept of this volume: locate and solve the technical problems first, then proceed. And for our present purposes I'll add that no one should have to spend time practicing non-music, or something that isn't particularly useful and that could, if misunderstood, cause harm.

If we take to heart the concepts outlined in this book, then there is no need to play all those well-meaning, yet misguided exercises we have inherited from the nineteenth century. Why misguided? Carl Czerny, Muzio Clementi and their ilk, outstanding pianists all—except, as we have learned, Hanon—played rather different instruments from those we play today. Well, fair enough. Those composers wrote studies for the instruments they knew. More importantly, though, they labored under serious misconceptions about how an efficient technique works, misconceptions that arose, at least in part, from techniques associated with the modern piano's forerunners, the harpsichord and *fortepiano*.

As we have seen, for Czerny and his colleagues, the technical emphasis was on "finger action," a "light hand," or a "quiet hand with fingers active to the utmost." These suggestions are among the few that Czerny offers in his collection of studies, *The Art of Finger Dexterity*. In a similar opus, *The School of Velocity*, the distinguished pedagogue leaves us no instruction at all. Likewise, Clementi abandons us to our own devices in his highly commercial *Gradus ad Parnassum* ("Steps to Parnassus"), the assumption being, I suppose, that we should provide our own technical knowhow. This begs the question, and yes I repeat myself, if we know how to play them correctly, then why study them at all?

A technique is practical when employing a process that saves time. I wonder if anyone has calculated the practice hours spent on exercises. (This would be an excellent dissertation topic for a doctoral candidate in pedagogy.) Time spent on exercises is a substitute for knowledge; it is a misguided attempt to develop technique without understanding what particular mechanisms are required. Have you ever tried to assemble a do-it-yourself kit by looking at the picture of the finished piece and allowing your intuition to guide you—only to get near the and find parts left over? It would have been better to read the instructions in order to get a sense of the whys and wherefores. If the instructions are in a foreign language, then you need a teacher.

A practical technique is one in which the pianist brings his knowledge to bear on each problematic passage. Knowledge—not an exercise in futility otherwise known as mindless rote. Knowledge—not a process of reaching to a shelf for a pre-packaged exercise, the author of which promises it will pave the way to Parnassus. Shall I say it one more time? We use our knowledge to solve technical issues in the music we want to play, not by first running a marathon or bench-pressing the 104 Broadway line loaded with rush hour commuters.

Personally, I don't believe Czerny hated little children. If you happen to have gone that route in your formative years, please don't be frightened that he may have hexed you. He hasn't. But, and this may come as a relief, you don't need to play him anymore if you don't want to. And if you do want to play him ,just know that, even though his exercises probably aren't carcinogenic, they are also not therapeutic. Put your Czerny and the others in the closet and turn the key. Put to use the concepts you've learned here and use the music itself for your studies.

ABOUT THE AUTHOR

Unlike life, playing the piano is easy and doesn't hurt. This mantra has carried the author through what might seem to others like several lifetimes—performing as a collaborative pianist, occasional soloist, symphony bassist and, through it all he has remained a dedicated teacher.

He took part in the first Taubman Institute at Rensselaerville, New York, and though he does not represent the Institute, he participated in many subsequent institutes at Amherst College while studying piano privately in New York with Edna Golandsky, who showed him that there are no mysteries regarding piano technique.

He has performed internationally with such artists as David Shifrin, Hermann Baumann, Eugenia Zukerman, Leona Mitchell, Clamma Dale and Christiane Edinger in venues from Vancouver to Boston and London to Moscow, including Carnegie Hall, the Kennedy Center, the White House, Vienna's Musikverein, Berlin's Hochschule and Tchaikovsky Hall in Moscow. He has played in the Great Performers at Lincoln Center series, the Berlin Festival, the Vienna Festival, Tage Neue Musik, Marlboro and the Newport Festival. His concertizing has taken him to every state in the contiguous United States. And yes, he has taught continuously.

After graduating *cum laude* from the University of Southern California, a scholarship student of Muriel Kerr, Jacob Gimpel and John Crown, he accepted a Naumberg scholarship on double bass to the Juilliard School (M.S.), during which time he performed in the American Symphony with Leopold Stokowski (Columbia Records) and in the Marlboro Festival Orchestra with Pablo Casals (Columbia Records). It was also during this time that he made his New York recital debut at Carnegie Recital Hall as a pianist with violinist Christiane Edinger. Later, he studied piano on a German government grant with Gerhard Puchelt in Berlin, completed a doctorate in piano at the University of Arizona with Nicholas Zumbro and for thirteen years taught applied piano at the University of Texas at El Paso, where he was a tenured professor. He now teaches privately in Los Angeles, writes, paints, takes photos of the world around him and plays cello in the Santa Monica Symphony.

SELECTED BIBLIOGRAPHY

Keller, Hermann. *Phrasing and Articulation: A Contribution to a Rhetoric of Music,* W.W. Morton & Co., Inc., New York, 1973.

Matthay, Tobias. *The Visible and Invisible in Pianoforte Technique*, Oxford University Press, 1932

Neuhaus, Heinrich. *The Art of Piano Playing,* Kahn & Averill, 1998 (Orig. Pub. 1958).

Ortmann, Otto. *The Physiological Mechanics of Piano Technique,* Dutton, 1962 (Orig. Pub. 1929).

Rosen, Charles. *The Classical Style: Haydn, Mozart, Beethoven*, W.W. Norton & Co., Inc., 1971.

Sándor, Gyögy. *On Piano Playing*, G. Schirmer Books, 1995

Stannard, Neil. *Piano Technique Demystified: Insights into Problem Solving*, CreatSpace.com, 2013.

Troeger, Richard. *Playing Bach on the Piano: A Practical Guide*, Amadeus Press, LLC, Cambridge, 2003.

INDEX

37549426R00076

Made in the USA
Middletown, DE
30 November 2016